1987
YEAR OF THE
SERIAL KILLER
CHAPTER 2

Ben Oakley

Twelve Trees

Hampshire, United Kingdom
hello@benoakley.co.uk

1987

YEAR OF THE SERIAL KILLER

CHAPTER 2

by Ben Oakley

Independently published.

ISBN: 9781707837601

Cover design by Marina Luisa

Discover more:

www.benoakley.co.uk

For Marina.

My soulmate & guardian angel.

Also by Ben Oakley

Non-fiction

The Monstrous Book of Serial Killers

1996: Year of the Serial Killer Chapter 3

1987: Year of the Serial Killer Chapter 2

1978: Year of the Serial Killer

The 'It Happened In...' Series

Mentacracy: Living under the Rule of Mental Illness

Fiction

Beyond the Blood Streams

Subnet: Final Contact

Subnet: Unknown Origin

Subnet: Alien Network

Stay up to date:

www.benoakley.co.uk

CHAPTERS

Introduction

After the success of *1978: Year of the Serial Killer*, published in May 2019, an effort was made to plan a worthy follow-up book. And we don't have to look very far for a year that was full to the brim of serial killers, cold cases, and true crime.

That year of course was **1987**.

Nine years after 1978, another year made from the same numbers stands out as the one with the most victims attributed to serial killers in any single year. Researchers at Radford University ascertained that there were 389 victims of serial killers in 1987.

That's 389 victims of serial killers in the United States alone. It doesn't include the hundreds from Europe and Russia and hundreds more from South America and Asia. 1987 was the year that serial killing broke records with the number of victims.

The number of victims in the United States has never been surpassed, in any year since. In comparison, 8 people were the victims of serial killers in Canada throughout the whole of 1987.

According to the Disaster Center; **20,096** people were murdered in the United States in 1987 alone. 25 people were executed in the United

States, and many arrested in 1987 would also be sentenced to death in the years that followed.

As with *1978: Year of the Serial Killer*, this book isn't about justifying serial killers or violent crime. It's about listing true crime within a timeline of a single year, and laying it all out in an easy-to-read format. The book is laid out in date order, to see connections where there were none before.

The final chapter lists 100 serial killers who were active in 1987 alone, formatted in an encyclopedic layout for easy reading. There are also another 200 events that have been added to the 1987 timeline for reference and cultural significance.

You'll also find snippets on unsolved murders, cold cases, mysterious disappearances, mass murders, spree killers, national disasters, assassinations, executions, and culturally significant world events. There are major discussion points, including; movies that influenced killers, the rise of DNA technology, and various unsolved serial killing sprees.

Every *Year of the Serial Killer* book is guaranteed to have information on over 100 serial killers. The book is fully researched and referenced, complete with appendices and a bibliography of all studies and data cited within these pages.

Three of the appendices at the back of the book are small sections that were also available in *1978: Year of the Serial Killer.* They have been added in addition due to their relevancy regarding 1987.

So how do we associate a serial killer with 1987?

They would have killed *in* 1987, meaning they have a confirmed or suspected murder victim in the twelve months from January 1st to December 31st.

They might have killed before *and* after 1987, meaning that someone could kill in 1986 *and* 1988 but are still considered *active* in 1987.

It includes serial killers who were arrested *in* 1987 but had killed victims in the years prior to their arrest. This means that up until their capture in 1987 they were still considered *active*.

Let's journey back to 1987, the age of mass consumerism and political violence. If 1978 was a masterpiece of murder, then 1987 is its big brother.

January 1987

January 1st

In Puerto Rico, 96 people are found dead after the *Dupont Plaza Hotel* fire in San Juan. It was an arson attack set by three angry employees of the hotel on the afternoon of December 31st 1986.

Most victims were unidentifiable due to the extreme fire that tore through the building. 84 bodies were found in the casino, five in the lobby, three in an elevator, and two near the pool outside of the hotel.

January 2nd

In Philadelphia, 23-year-old *Deborah Dudley* is kidnapped by rapist and murderer *Gary Michael Heidnik*. She was held captive and murdered on March 19th, 1987. In less than six months from November 1986 to March 1987, Heidnik had kidnapped, tortured, and raped six African-American women.

He would keep them prisoner in a pit in the basement of his home and would go on to kill two of them. Another victim; 24-year-old *Sandra Lindsay*, was kidnapped on December 3rd 1986, and killed in February of

1987. She died of starvation and the effects of torture. Heidnik went on to dismember her body, cook her ribs in an oven and boil her head.

It was suggested he may have minced the flesh, mixed it with dog food and fed it to his other victims but those reports remain uncorroborated. Heidnik was arrested on March 24th 1987, after a new captive managed to call for help. He was sentenced to death and executed by lethal injection in July 1999.

January 4th

In Baltimore County, Maryland, one of America's worst rail disasters kills 16 people and injures 164. An *Amtrak* train carrying 660 passengers crashed into a set of locomotives at 108 miles per hour.

The *Conrail* locomotive crew had failed to stop at signals and later tested positive for marijuana use. The engineer served only four years for negligence. At the time it was the worst crash in Amtrak's history until a 1993 disaster killed 47 people.

January 6th

In North Carolina, 23-year-old *Kimberly Ann Ruggles* was raped, robbed, and murdered by American serial killer *Ronald Adrin Gray*. Gray was just 20-years-old at the time and had recently joined the U.S. Army in 1984. He had been stationed at Fort Bragg in North Carolina, a year before the murder.

Gray would go on to receive four convictions of murder and eight counts of rape. His crimes were committed while he was a serving soldier and so he was sentenced to death by a military court. He went on to receive stays of execution multiple times in the years that followed.

As of 2019, he remains on death row while further investigations take place.

On the same day.

Astronomers witness the birth of a giant galaxy during its formation stages for the first time in human history. The galaxy was 12 billion light years from Earth, which was said to have been an early moment in the history of the Universe.

January 7th

In South Africa, the body of 10-year-old *Yussuf Hoffmann* was discovered. He had been raped and strangled to death with a piece of his own clothing. His hands were tied behind his back and his face had been pushed into the sand in the area of Rocklands.

He was a victim of South African serial killer *Norman Simons* who killed at least 22 young boys between 1986 and 1994. On April 13th, 1994, Norman Simons was arrested in connection with another murdered boy who had been discovered on the now infamous *Weltevrede Dunes*; his dumping ground of choice.

He was sentenced to life for the murder of one of the victims but is claimed to have killed at least 21 more. He is currently incarcerated at the *Drakenstein Maximum Correctional Facility* in Paarl, the same prison were *Nelson Mandela* was imprisoned.

January 8th

In Pennsylvania, the body of *Jeanne Durkin* is discovered beneath a storage truck just off of Frankford Avenue. She had been stabbed 74 times and was found in a pool of blood. She was naked from the waist down and had been positioned in a provocative position.

Durkin was a homeless woman who was most commonly seen sleeping in the doorway just a few numbers down from *Goldie's Bar*. She was a victim of *The Frankford Slasher*, an unidentified serial killer in the Frankford area of Philadelphia. Although one person was convicted of one of the killings, the murders have never been solved.

January 9th

A hold-over from the 1970s, *Charles Manson* is interviewed at *San Quentin Prison*. The interview is aired on January 27th on the NBC network in the United States. Manson would give two interviews to NBC and LIFE Magazine to promote a book written about him from an ex-convict who had conversed with him.

"I've never killed anyone. Maybe I should have killed 400 or 500 people. Then I would have felt better."

Manson was sentenced to death 16 years earlier but California's death penalty law was struck down and his sentence was commuted life in prison.

'Believe me, if I started murdering people there'd be none of you left.'

Charles Manson in his interview.

January 10th

In South Korea, 19-year-old *Hong Jin-young* is found murdered. She is a victim of the unsolved *Hwaseong Serial Murders*. At least ten females between the age of 14-years-old to 71-years-old were found tied, raped, and strangled with their own clothing. The murders took place between 1986 and 1991 and remain unsolved to this day. A list of over 21,000 suspects has been put together over the years.

Serial killing is rare in South Korea, or at the least not brought into the public eye. This is one of the only cases where a killer using the same modus operandi had been identified in the country. Because of the ridiculous notion of statute of limitations, the killings could not be investigated after 2006 but police still keep records due to the infamy of the case.

Statute of limitations means that there is a maximum time limit placed on crimes for when legal proceedings can be brought to an individual. Many Western countries have a statute of limitations. The United Kingdom is the exception in that there is no current time limit in place.

On the same day.

In Stratton, Vermont, a 38-year-old nurse named *Barbara Agnew* was stabbed to death in her car during a snowstorm. She had been returning from a skiing trip but never made it home. A snowplow driver found the car at a rest stop and went to see if the driver needed assistance.

The window was cracked and blood covered the steering wheel but there was no one inside. Agnew wouldn't be discovered until March 28th 1987. Her body was found beside an apple tree in Windsor County.

She was a victim of a serial killer known as the *Connecticut River Valley Killer*. The unidentified killer is suggested to have been responsible for at least seven murders in and around Claremont, New Hampshire, and the Connecticut River Valley area.

On the same day.

In Los Angeles, the body of 23-year-old *Barbara Ware* is discovered in Central-Alameda. She had died at the hands of LA-based serial killer *Lonnie David Franklin Jr.* When he was arrested in 2010 he had claimed at least ten victims but is suspected and linked to a possible 25.

Franklin killed seven people from 1985 to 1988 but then came a 14 year gap when there were no killings. He then killed again three more times from 2002 to 2007. The gap between the killings earned him the notorious moniker of *The Grim Sleeper*.

January 15th

In Brixton, London, *Inspector Douglas Lovelock*, who shot and paralysed a mother-of-six in a confused police raid in 1985, was cleared of all criminal charges. The shooting caused violent riots in Brixton which led to the death of a photographer and injured over 50 people. Lovelock was reinstated shortly after being cleared of all wrong-doing.

January 17th

In the United States, a soldier from Fort Bragg discovered the decomposing body of 18-year-old *Laura Lee Vickery-Clay*, who had disappeared from Fort Bragg a month earlier. She had been raped, beaten and shot multiple times. The murder weapon was found just a few yards from her body.

She was murdered by American serial killer *Ronald Adrin Gray*, who was an acting soldier at Fort Bragg. His fingerprints were found in Vickery-Clay's car. Gray was convicted on four counts of murder and eight counts of rape. He was sentenced to death by a military court and received stays of execution multiple times.

As of 2019, he remains on death row while further investigations take place.

January 19th

Australian serial killer *Lindsey Robert Rose* broke into a house in the West Ryde area of New South Wales. It was the home of *William Graf*, a known businessman. Rose had intended to rob the property of some of the more pricer belongings but he was caught in the act by Graf's partner; *Reynette Holford*.

Rose then stabbed Reynette multiple times with a screwdriver and a vegetable knife. He tied her up after he had attacked her, before running from the property. Reynette was left to die of her injuries. Rose was caught ten years later in 1997 and was convicted of five murders between 1984 and 1994.

As of 2019, he remains in prison serving five consecutive life sentences.

January 20th

English hostage negotiator *Terry Waite* was taken hostage and held for 1,763 days. Born Terrence Hardy Waite, he travelled to Lebanon as an envoy for the *Church of England* to try to secure the release of four hostages.

He met the captors of the hostages only to be held captive himself. Of the 1,763 days, four years were spent in solitary confinement. He was released back to the United Kingdom on November 18th 1991. He has since become a humanitarian and author.

January 22nd

The day the Republican shot himself dead on national television. The 30th State Treasurer of the Commonwealth of Pennsylvania; *Robert Budd Dwyer,* killed himself in front of a live audience. A year earlier, Dwyer was convicted of receiving a bribe from a Californian company that won a contract to get compensation for state workers who had overpaid taxes in error.

He was set to have been sentenced on January 23rd 1987. On the 22nd, he called a press conference in Harrisburg, Pennsylvania, and waited for the crowd of reporters to gather. Then he shot himself in the mouth with a Magnum Revolver. His suicide was then broadcast to a wide television audience across the state.

On the same day.

In Manila, Philippines, *The Mendiola Massacre*, AKA; *Black Thursday,* takes place. At Mendiola in Manila, state security forces violently disrupt a farmers march which had been organised to protest at the lack of government action on land reform. The forces opened fire killing at least 13 people and injuring over 50 protesters. 23 security force members were also injured.

January 23rd

In South Africa, the body of 13-year-old *Mario Thomas* was discovered in Kuilsriver, less than 20 miles away from the location of the body of *Yussuf Hoffmann* who was discovered on January 7th. Like Hoffman, Thomas had been raped and strangled to death with a piece of his own clothing.

He was one of 22 victims of South African serial killer *Norman Simons* who was active between 1986 and 1994. He is considered to be one of South Africa's worst known serial killers.

January 25th

In Los Angeles, 24-year-old *Loretta Perry* was found dead in a housing block. She had been raped and murdered by serial killer *Louis Craine*. At around the same time, a number of black serial killers were active in the Los Angeles region and two of Louis Craine's murders were previously attributed to *The Southside Slayer*.

Almost all of the victims were young black women who were either prostitutes or drug users. The bodies would be dumped in remote parks, in alleys, or in vacant buildings.

In 1989, Craine was arrested and sentenced to death for the murders of four women. He was acquitted in the trial of the fifth victim but it has since been attributed to him. Within months of his conviction, he died in a prison hospital of unknown natural causes.

January 31st

In the United States, the longest film ever made at the time premieres in its entirety at *The School of the Art Institute of Chicago*. It was the 85 hour long '*The Cure for Insomnia*', directed by *John Henry Timmis IV*. The film has no plot, and consists of artist *L. D. Groban* reading his 4,080 page poem; *A Cure for Insomnia*, over the course of three days.

It is edited to include clips of heavy metal music videos and pornographic images. It has never been released on DVD or other home video formats and all known copies are considered as lost.

The Frankford Slasher

The Frankford Slasher is a moniker for a serial killer who was active in and around the Frankford region of Philadelphia, in Pennsylvania, from 1985 to 1990. A black man named *Leonard Christopher* was convicted for one of the nine linked victims. He was convicted on minimal evidence and most witnesses saw the victims with a middle-aged white man before their deaths. All of the victims were sexually assaulted and stabbed to death.

On August 26th 1985, the body of 52-year-old *Helen Patent* was found by transit workers at a train yard in Philadelphia. She had been left half-naked and laid out in a provocative manner. She had been stabbed 47 times and her organs had been exposed by the vicious attack.

On January 3rd 1986, only a few miles from the first victim, the brutalised body of *Anna Carroll* was found on the floor of her bedroom. She too had been left nude and in a provocative position. She had been stabbed six times and had been gutted, exposing her insides. The kitchen knife used in the attack was left inside of her.

After a third victim was discovered on Christmas Day, 1986, investigators began to make connections. All three victims had been regulars at the *Goldie's Bar* on Frankford Avenue. The area had been well known for drug users and had a reputation as a big nightlife centre.

On January 8th 1987, the body of *Jeanne Durkin* was discovered beneath a storage truck just off of Frankford Avenue. She had been stabbed 74 times and was found in a pool of her own blood. She was naked from the waist down and had also been positioned in a provocative position. Durkin was a homeless woman who was commonly seen sleeping in an entranceway just a few doors down from Goldie's Bar. It was then that investigators realised a serial killer was at large.

They informed the media that the crimes were not related and the killings stopped for an entire year. Until January 1988 when 66-year-old *Margaret Vaughan* was found murdered in a similar fashion to the previous four victims. They created a sketch of the murderer who had been seen drinking with her in Goldie's Bar, and asked the public for help.

Another year passed and another victim was found in January of 1989. 30-year-old *Theresa Sciortino* was found in her apartment just outside of the Frankford region of the city. She had been stabbed 25 times and was found on the kitchen floor in a pool of her own blood.

Her wounds had been caused by a kitchen knife which was left at the scene. Next to her body was a three-foot section of wood that had been used to sexually violate her with. Investigators discovered that she was also a regular at the Goldie's Bar.

Another year passed and yet another body turned up on April 19th 1990. The body of *Carol Dowd* was discovered in an alley near a fish market. She had been raped and stabbed 36 times. Due to the brutality of the attack, her intestines had spilled out of her body. Then a connection was made between Dowd and two of the previous victims; Sciortino and Durkin. They had all been in and out of psychiatric wards in the years prior to their murders.

Upon interviewing some of the fish market employees they met with Leonard Christopher who worked there and lived in the area. He said that he knew one of the victims; Margaret Vaughan. Because he did not have an alibi, he was arrested on May 5th 1990 and charged with Dowd's murder.

Witness stories were all over the place, some placed him at the scene of the crime, while others said he was of good character and was nowhere near the murder scenes. On June 20th 1990, Christopher stood trial for the murder of Carol Dowd as the evidence was deemed sufficient enough.

His description didn't fit the one given by witnesses for the other murders but on December 12th 1990, Christopher was sentenced to life for the murder of Dowd. The evidence was circumstantial at best but it didn't matter. Not even when another body was found.

Two months earlier on September 6th, while Christopher was in prison awaiting trial, the body of 30-year-old *Michelle Denher* was found in her apartment just one block away from Frankford. She had been raped and stabbed 23 times. Her body had been found in a provocative position and she had a large slash to her stomach which exposed her intestines.

Astonishingly, Denher was also a psychiatric patient, who lived just three blocks away from the previous murder, and also drank in Goldie's Bar. A day before her murder, she had been seen with a middle-aged white man who fitted the original description of The Frankford Slasher.

The public were not convinced that Christopher had killed Dowd, and so the story had caught the attention of local media and community groups. One theory even pointed to witchcraft, due to a cult presence in the area that held rituals in a local park.

Investigators have since claimed there is no evidence that pointed to Christopher being The Frankford Slasher. As of 2019, the eight other murders are now part of an active cold case.

Leonard Christopher has since died of cancer.

Ahmad Suradji – *The Black Magic Killer*

In Indonesia, *Ahmad Suradji, AKA: The Black Magic Killer*, killed at least 42 young girls and women between 1986 and 1997. He became known by many names, including *Dukan AS, Nasib Kelewang, Datuk Maringgi*, or *The Sorcerer*.

Suradji's victims were between the ages of 11-years-old to 30-years-old and were part of an ongoing ritual that saw him requiring 70 victims. He strangled them and buried them in the ground up to their waists, on his sugar cane plantation. He *planted* them in such a way that their heads were facing his house, believing their positions imbibed him with extra powers.

He lived in Medan, in the North Sumatran region of Indonesia, where he worked as a cattle-breeder. He claimed to be a *dukun*, which is a class of shaman who are supposed to hold supernatural powers. He assisted local women on how to find fortune and how to keep their beauty.

In 1986, Suradji's deceased father visited him in a dream and commanded him to murder 70 females as part of a larger black magic ritual. Believing it to be a real commandment, he began his campaign of murder. He married three sisters, who lived with him on the plantation and appeased his every need. Upon his arrest, they were also arrested on conspiracy to murder as accomplices.

He told them of the visitation from his father and what needed to be done. He claimed that by killing 70 women, he would become even more powerful and be able to perform more elaborate and compelling acts of supernatural magic, including becoming a mystical healer. Although he was linked to 42 murders, there were reports at the time that over 80 people had gone missing in the area and that he may have reached his target of 70.

In 1997, a 21-year-old girl named *Sri Kemala Dewi*, was dropped off by a rickshaw driver at the home of the datuk healer. Three days later, her naked body was discovered in a sugar cane field. The rickshaw driver told police that he had dropped her off at the home of Suradji. Upon visiting the property, they found items belonging to the victim, including her handbag.

On April 30th 1997, Suradji was arrested. He confessed to her murder and the murders of at least 42 other females in the same manner. When the investigation turned to excavating the sugar cane plantation, 42 bodies were found with some so far along the decomposition process that they could not be identified.

He claimed his father's ghost told him to drink the saliva of 70 dead women to reach the level of power that he wanted to have. He said it would have taken too many lifetimes to encounter 70 dead women and so he decided to kill in order to drink their saliva and speed up the process of gaining more magical powers.

"My father did not specifically advise me to kill people. So I was thinking, it would take ages if I have to wait to get seventy women. I was trying to get to it as fast as possible, I took my own initiative to kill."

He chose victims from the women that came to visit him for spiritual guidance and magical assistance. Enough women were coming to him but when he had a gap with no victims, he purposely went out to seek prostitutes and homeless women. Word spread around local villages of his healing powers, so more and more people came his way to gain advice or assistance.

Before he would give guidance, or healing, he charged each of his victims the going rate for the ritual which was approximately $200 USD. For those who wanted to be more sexually attractive to men, he would charge more. Once he had the money in hand, he led them to the deaths.

He took them into the nearby sugar cane fields where he had the victims dig their own graves before burying them up to their waist. They believed it was all part of a magical healing ritual. When they couldn't move out of the mud, he then strangled them until they were dead and drank the saliva from their mouths. Then he removed the clothes of the victims and buried them back in the ground with their heads facing his house.

Suradji's three wives were investigated after the murders were discovered but only one was charged as his accomplice. *Tumini* went on trial at the same time as Suradji. She received the death penalty but it was later commuted to life in prison. His other two wives had no knowledge of the murders or ritual.

"The black magic came from God. I don't have it anymore, I have repented. I hope I have a chance to live."

Suradji – in a final interview.

Suradji was sentenced to death and was executed by firing squad on July 10th 2008. He was allowed one last liaison with his convicted wife, Tumini, before he was led out to the firing range.

February 1987

February 1st

In Minneapolis, the body of 81-year-old *Lillian Kuller* is discovered in her apartment by another tenant, with a pillow over her face. She had been strangled and beaten to death during a robbery.

In 2017, a cold-case investigation which had opened in 2010, finally solved the murder. DNA on Kuller's fingernails and clothes, which had been in storage for 23 years was re-administered to the investigation and the culprit was found. The DNA matched serial robber *Michael Anthony Withers,* who was already in prison on 12 convictions of aggravated robbery between 1985 and 2014.

After 31 years, Withers was finally convicted for Kuller's murder. On October 30th 2018, he received a sentence of 20 years in prison.

February 5th

In California, drifter killer *Dennis Duane Webb* broke into the home of *John Rainwater* and his wife, Lori, who had just returned home with her five-day-old son. Webb tied both of them up, then raped and beat both of them all night. After he was finished, he shot them to death with a bullet in the back of their heads.

Webb was known as a racist drifter who travelled across the Southern States with outlaw motorcycle gangs. He killed his first victim in 1973 because the man was gay – there was no other motive. He went on to kill another man as part of a gang initiation and then he assassinated a male target as ordered by the gang.

In 1988 he was convicted of the Rainwater murders and sentenced to death. In 2016, while on death row at San Quentin Prison in California, he died of natural causes.

February 7th

Roberta Joseph Hayes, 21-years-old, disappears without a trace. Her body is discovered on September 11th, 1991. She is one of 48 confirmed victims of serial killer, *Gary Ridgeway,* AKA*: The Green River Killer*.

February 8th

In California, 15-year-old pregnant prostitute *Tracy Clark* was found shot to death in a canal near Lamont in Kern County. She had been killed by *David Keith Rogers*, a U.S. Navy veteran who then worked for the Kern County Sheriff's Department.

A year earlier, 21-year-old Los Angeles prostitute *Jeanine Benintende* was pulled out of the same canal. She too had been shot multiple times. The bullets were identified as being from the same gun and belonging to Rogers. He had been briefly fired from the department in 1983 for photographing naked prostitutes in cemeteries. But an appeal saw him return to active duty.

He was arrested on February 13th 1987, and subsequently sentenced to death. The investigation discovered his dark fascination with prostitutes along with vast amounts of pornographic material in his home. He was also linked to at least three other murders of prostitutes in the area from 1983 to 1987.

On July 15th, 2019, Rogers filed an appeal for his death sentence to be reduced to life.

February 10th

In Lupao, Philippines, the *Lupao Massacre* takes place. The Army killed suspected members of the *New People's Army* at a town near the base of the Carabello mountain range. An Army Lieutenant was killed and at least eight others were wounded.

On the same day.

German-Italian serial killing duo, *Wolfgang Abel and Marco Furlan* are sentenced to 30 years each. They participated in the murders of at least 10 victims from 1977 to 1984, in Germany, Italy, and the Netherlands.

It was suggested that between them they may have claimed up to 28 victims. At each crime scene they left a leaflet written in Italian, it showed a Nazi Eagle and swastika and each of them had a different slogan. *"We are the last of the Nazis"* and *"Death comes to those who betray the true god"* being two of them.

They were caught in 1984, and Furlan was subsequently released in

2010. Abel was moved to house arrest and then finally released to live amongst us in 2016.

February 11th

The United States, under *Operation Musketeer*, carries out a six kiloton nuclear test at the Nevada test site. It is exploded in an underground shaft and codenamed; *Tornero*, which is Italian for '*I'll be back*'.

February 13th

In Robertson County, California, 72-year-old *Alice Martin* was abducted by American serial killer *Daniel Lee Corwin* whilst out walking near her home. Her body was found the next day in a field. She had been raped before being strangled and stabbed to death.

Corwin was subsequently convicted of three 1987 murders, sentenced to death and executed by lethal injection in December of 1988.

February 20th

A bomb planted by the *Unabomber* explodes and injures computer store worker *Gary Wright*. The bomb was disguised as a piece of wood and Wright attempted to remove it from the store's parking lot. In doing so he set it off and he was left with over 200 pieces of shrapnel in his body.

The Unabomber, *Theodore 'Ted' Kaczynski*, was an American terrorist and a mathematics prodigy. From 1978 to 1995, he killed three people and injured 23 more in an attempt to begin a revolution. His efforts found him targeting people and companies involved with modern technology.

As of 2019, Kaczynski remains incarcerated at the supermax *ADX Florence* Prison in Colorado.

February 22nd

In America, world-renowned creative *Andy Warhol* dies from an irregular heartbeat following an operation. He became a leading figure in the art movement that became known as *pop art*. He died at 58-years-old in the New York hospital where he had been recovering from gallbladder surgery.

Accused of improper care and suggested water intoxication, Warhol's family sued the hospital. They then settled out of court for an undisclosed sum of money. Warhol's legacy is evident in art movements today and there have been numerous films and documentaries about his life.

February 24th

In Chile, the *SN 1987A Supernova* became the first observable supernova to be seen with the naked-eye from Earth since 1604. It was discovered independently by *Ian Shelton* and *Oscar Duhalde* at the *Las Campanas Observatory* in Chile.

SN 1987A was 168,000 light years away and was located in the *Large Magellanic Cloud* dwarf galaxy. The supernova occurred when a massive star collapsed and exploded. It destroyed the star and sent out shock waves that may have birthed new stars and worlds through the huge release of energy that it created.

Due to its proximity to Earth and the timing of its discovery, it has become one of the most studied events in the history of astronomy.

Gary Ridgway – *The Green River Killer*

Gary Ridgway, AKA: *The Green River Killer*, was an American serial killer who was convicted of 48 murders and has been linked to many more since. He is one of the country's most prolific killers who killed teenage girls and women in Washington State.

Born *Gary Leon Ridgway* in 1949, a few years after the end of World War Two. He was raised in a home of violent arguments and hatred for a mother who had a dominant personality. His father was a bus driver, and it is claimed he constantly moaned about the large number of sex workers he would see on any given shift.

Ridgway later claimed that he felt a sexual attraction to his mother and as such often fantasised about killing her. Up until the age of 13-years-old, Ridgway was a regular bed-wetter. The humiliation only continued as his mother would make a point of washing his genitals afterwards.

Bed-wetting is one of the elements of the *Macdonald Triad*, which cites three factors during childhood that may be markers to violence later on in life. These include bed-wetting, harm to animals, and setting fires. First proposed by psychiatrist *J.M. Macdonald* in 1963, it has since evolved to various different factors associated with childhood behaviour and later violence.

When Ridgway was 16-years-old, after being held back for a year in school, he lured another pupil into the woods and stabbed him. The boy survived and Ridgway went unpunished. In 1969 he married his 19-year-old girlfriend and then joined the U.S. Navy. He was subsequently sent to Vietnam where he was involved in combat. While he was in Vietnam, his wife cheated on him and their marriage ended within 12 months.

But Ridgway wasn't any less innocent at the time, he had encounters with various prostitutes while in the military. The resulting under-achievement of the Vietnam War, infected the national psyche like a plague. Personal failure, wasted lives, national failure, and a divide that reached the political parties.

Most of the American military were drinking lots of alcohol or doing drugs. Some took part in violent rapes and senseless murders. Most were psychologically affected by their experiences. They all came back to the United States and brought their psychological disturbances with them.

Ridgway's second marriage ended in a similar manner with his wife cheating on him. During that time, he found God and fell into religion in a big way, taking part in sermons and reading the bible daily. Regardless of his religion, he continued to use the services of sex workers, due to an insatiable appetite for sexual contact.

There was a very clear paradox at work; Ridgway hated the presence of prostitutes in his area but would use their services more and more as time went on. Soon he began to hate them so much that he refused to pay them.

"I picked prostitutes as my victims because I hate most prostitutes and I did not want to pay them for sex."

His first victim was in 1982, 16-year-old *Wendy Lee Coffield*. Ridgway would earn the trust of a prostitute by showing a picture of his son, before either taking them home, to his truck, or to a secluded area. Then he would rape them and strangle them from behind. For a while he used his hands to kill them but moved to using a ligature to prevent any bruising to himself.

From 1982 to 1998, and possibly a little after, he had killed at least 71 teenage girls and women. In the early 1980s, the *King County Sheriff's Office* created the *Green River Task Force* to investigate the murders.

Two task force members; *Robert Keppel* and Dave *Reichert*, had famously interviewed *Ted Bundy* in 1984. And it was Bundy himself who offered a profile on The Green River Killer.

He suggested the killer was revisiting the burial or dumping sites to have sex with his victims. He said that if police found a fresh grave, then they should stake it out and wait for him to come back.

Astonishingly, Ridgway *would* return to the places where he dumped the bodies. He dumped the bodies in '*clusters*', mostly in wooded areas. He would return to the bodies to engage in acts of necrophilia with the corpses.

He later claimed that having sex with a corpse stopped him from killing someone else at that very moment.

"I placed most of the bodies in groups which I call clusters. I did this because I wanted to keep track of all the women I killed. I liked to drive by the clusters around the county and think about the women I placed there."

He married again in 1988 and claimed to have loved her more than anything. In the time after his third marriage, he only killed a suspected three more victims until his final arrest in 2001. DNA samples collected in 1987 proved to be vital to his arrest.

At his trial in 2003, he entered a plea bargain to plead guilty to 48 charges of murder instead of the seven he was originally charged with. This allowed the families of 41 more victims to find resolution. He claimed more murders and is linked to at least 71 in total. He was sentenced to life in prison, and as of 2019 is currently incarcerated at the *High Security Federal Prison* in Florence, Colorado.

He is constantly being made available for information relating to open murder investigations and remains one of the most notorious serial killers in the United States.

March 1987

March 1st

The '*Murder She Wrote*' episode; *Simon Says, Color Me Dead*, airs for the first time. In it, Jessica (Angela Lansbury) investigates a case where an artist is murdered and his prized painting is missing.

Murder She Wrote first aired on the *CBS Network* in the United States from 1984 until 1996, and consisted of 264 episodes. Eight of its 12 seasons ended in the top ten for their respective years. At its peak, in the late-1980s, the series played to over 40 million viewers.

March 6th

The *Zebrugge Disaster* shocks Europe. The *MS Herald of Free Enterprise* was a ferry which capsized moments after leaving the Belgian port of Zeebrugge. The ferry was headed to the English port of Dover.

The ship was an eight-deck car and passenger ferry that had been designed for rapid loading and unloading. When the ship left the port, the bow-door had remained open, and water flooded the decks. Just minutes later, the ship was on its side.

The ship was carrying 459 passengers and 80 crew. The entire incident from taking on water to capsizing took only 90 seconds. The water instantly flooded the ships systems and destroyed all emergency power leaving it in darkness. It was only when a nearby dredger noticed the lights had disappeared that they notified the authorities. The alarm was raised over ten minutes later.

Rescue helicopters and the *Belgian Navy* assisted in the rescue. A nearby German ferry captain risked his own life and ship to save people from the water. He was later given a medal from *King Baudouin* of Belgium for his heroism. Most of the victims were British who were taking advantage of cheap travel to the continent.

Many victims were trapped inside the ship and died of hypothermia. Those bodies that were recoverable were removed in the days that followed. The sinking of *MS Herald of Free Enterprise* resulted in the highest death-count of any peacetime maritime disaster involving a British ship since 1919.

The disaster killed 193 passengers and crew.

On the same day.

In Ecuador, a series of earthquakes kill over 1,000 people with 4,000 left missing. The three quakes happened over a six-hour period, measuring 6.7, 7.1, and 6.0 on the Richter scale. The epicentres ranged from the Andes to just north of the *Reventador Volcano*. Along with the massive loss of life, the quakes caused over one billion dollars worth (USD) of damage.

March 7th

At Donggang Bay, in Fujian, China, the *Donggang Massacre* or *Lieyu Massacre* takes place. The *Republic of China Army* executed unarmed Vietnamese refugees in a fishing boat. They were seeking political asylum when they were shot at. At least 19 people were killed. The superior officers involved received no official punishment for the murders.

March 9th

In Los Angeles, 21-year-old *Diane Johnson* is murdered by American serial killer, *Chester Dewayne Turner*, AKA: *The Southside Slayer*. The victim was linked with DNA evidence provided by police and he was arrested in 2003.

In 2007, Turner was first convicted of killing 10 women from 1987 to 1998, in addition to the death of an unborn child. By 2014 he was convicted of another four murders, bringing his total to 15 victims, and suspected of many more. He received death sentences in both trials and currently remains on death row.

March 10th

In Sydenham, London, Private Investigator *Daniel John Morgan* was killed with an axe to the head. His body was found beside his vehicle in a pub car park, his watch had been stolen but his wallet and a wad of cash had not been touched. It left investigators with the impression the robbery had been staged to look like the reason for the murder.

Reports at the time stated that he was close to exposing police corruption within the *Metropolitan Police Service*. In 2011, the murder was at the centre of the *News of the World* scandal involving journalist misconduct.

As of 2019, his murder still remains unsolved but has been the subject of many failed police inquiries, and is the basis for conspiracy theories to this day.

March 14th

In Switzerland, the body of 16-year-old *Vincent Puippe*, is discovered near Valais. He had been tied, beaten and raped, before his corpse was burned. He was a victim of Swiss serial killer *Michel Peiry*, AKA: the *Sadist of Romont*.

Piery would abduct or lure teenage hitchhikers then tie them up and rape or abuse them. Afterwards he would violently murder them and burn the bodies. He killed 11 hitchhikers between 1981 and 1987, and is said to be the worst in the country since World War Two.

As of 2019, he remains in prison in Switzerland, serving a life sentence.

March 16th

Ukrainian female serial killer *Tamara Ivanyutina* poisoned the canteen food at a school where she worked. Two pupils and two adults were killed and nine others went to intensive care. After an investigation led to her arrest shortly after, she confessed to further murders all the way back to 1976.

Ivanyutina killed nine people over an 11-year period. As most female serial killers tend to do, she used poisoning as her modus operandi. She used thallium to poison people she simply didn't like. She claimed she targeted the school canteen because the sixth-graders refused to set up tables and chairs, and so she decided to punish them.

She was executed by firing squad later in 1987.

March 17th

The body of 20-year-old soldier, *Darlene Krashoc*, was found behind a Korean Club Restaurant, she had been strangled to death. Krashoc had been stationed at *Fort Carson*. For over 30 years, her murder remained unsolved.

That was until June 2019, when Colorado Springs cold case homicide investigators and *Army Criminal Investigation Command* arrested a 58-year-old man. He has recently been charged with the murder, having been caught using genetic genealogy DNA analysis.

The trial is pending and will be updated in a later edition of the book.

On the same day.

In Finland, serial killer *Jukka Torsten Lindholm*, was found guilty of two charges of manslaughter among other crimes. He was sentenced to just over nine years. Upon his release he would go on to kill others.

His crimes began in his teenage years and showed no signs of letting up. In 1981, when he was just 16-years-old, he abducted a 16-year-old girl and dragged her into a basement where he beat and choked her. The girl escaped and identified Lindholm as the attacker.

He was sent to a youth prison in 1984 for one year for various other attacks and thefts. In 1985, upon his release, he killed his 48-year-old mother in the apartment they shared. Despite being a suspect, he was not charged with the murder.

In July of 1986, he lured two 12-year-old girls to his apartment for alcohol. He locked one of the girls in the bathroom as he choked the other one to death. When he released the girl in the bathroom, he raped and beat her but she escaped and ran from the apartment. Lindholm was caught shortly after whilst hiding out in a forest.

From 1985 to 2018, he had killed at least four people and had attacked and raped numerous others. He is Finland's worst known serial killer.

March 18th

In Los Angeles, the body of *Vivian Collins* was found in an abandoned house in the 1600 block of *East Century Boulevard* in the neighbourhood of Watts.

She had been raped and murdered by serial killer *Louis Craine*. Craine was sentenced to death for Perry's killing and the killing of three other women. Within months of his conviction, he died in a prison hospital of unknown natural causes.

In 1989, Craine was arrested and sentenced to death for the murders of four women. He was acquitted in the trial of the fifth victim but it has since been attributed to him.

On the same day.

The United States, under *Operation Musketeer*, carry out a 3.5 kiloton nuclear test at the Nevada test site. It is exploded in an underground tunnel and codenamed; *Middle Note.*

March 19th

In Sacramento, the body of 18-year-old prostitute *Maria Apodaca* is discovered. She had been bound, wrapped up in bedding and then buried. She had been raped and killed by American serial killer; *Morris Solomon Jr.* AKA: *The Sacramento Slayer.* Solomon is currently on death row at San Quentin, after being convicted of six murders. He is linked to at least one more.

March 21st

In California, the son of Hollywood legend *Dean Martin* is killed on a routine training mission in his F-4 Jet Fighter. *Dean Paul Martin Jr.* took off from *March Air Force Base* and crashed in the San Bernardino Mountains during a snowstorm, killing him and his weapons systems officer. He was a member of the *California Air National Guard*, a pop singer and up-and-coming film and television actor.

March 28th

In Windsor County, Vermont, the body of 38-year-old nurse *Barbara Agnew* was discovered beside an apple tree. Her car had been found in a snowstorm on January 10th 1987, the window was cracked and there was blood on the steering wheel.

She had been stabbed to death by the *Connecticut River Valley Killer*. The unidentified killer is suggested to have been responsible for at least seven murders in and around Claremont, New Hampshire, and the Connecticut River Valley area.

March 29ᵗʰ

In Hollywood, the *7th Golden Raspberry Awards* are held at the *Hollywood Roosevelt Hotel*. It awarded the worst films from 1986. For the first time, the Razzies had a tie for Worst Picture, between *Howard the Duck* and *Under the Cherry Moon*.

Worst Actor award went to *Prince* for *Under the Cherry Moon*, Worst Actress award went to *Madonna* for *Shanghai Surprise*. The Worst Career Achievement award went to *Bruce the Rubber Shark* from *Jaws* (1975), *Jaws 2* (1978) and *Jaws 3-D* (1983).

March 30ᵗʰ

In the United Kingdom, *Harold Shipman* kills his first of eight victims in 1987 alone. He kills 76-year-old *Frank Halliday* from Dukinfield. Also known as Doctor Death, Shipman was one of the most prolific serial killers in history. He was found guilty of 215 murders of patients under his care but is linked to over 250.

On the same day.

In Los Angeles, the *59th Academy Awards* took place at the *Dorothy Chandler Pavilion*. The Best Picture award went to Oliver Stone's *Platoon*, he also won Best Director for the movie.

Best Actor went to *Paul Newman* for *The Color of Money*, and Best Actress went to *Marlee Matlin* for *Children of a Lesser God*. *Platoon* won four Oscars. *Hannah and Her Sisters* and *A Room With a View* won three Oscars, and *Aliens* won two Oscars.

The Connecticut River Valley Killer

The *Connecticut River Valley Killer* is a suspected and as yet unidentified serial killer who is linked to at least seven murders on the New Hampshire and Vermont border. The murders were over a nine-year period from 1978 to 1987.

On January 10th 1987, In Stratton, Vermont, a 38-year-old nurse named *Barbara Agnew* was stabbed to death in her car during a snowstorm. She had been returning from a skiing trip but never made it home. A snowplow driver found the car at a rest stop and went to see if the driver needed assistance.

The window was cracked and blood covered the steering wheel, but there was no one inside. Agnew wouldn't be discovered until March 28th 1987. Her body was found beside an apple tree in Windsor County.

On October 24th 1978, 27-year-old *Cathy Millican* was seen photographing birds at the *Chandler Brook Wetland Preserve* in New London, New Hampshire. The next day, her body was found only a few feet away from where she had been seen. She had been stabbed 29 times.

On July 25th 1981, 37-year-old student *Mary Elizabeth Critchley*, disappeared while hitchhiking near *Interstate 91* at the Massachusetts and Vermont border. Two weeks later, her body was discovered in a wooded area in New Hampshire. Due to the viciousness of the attack and exposure to the elements, the coroner was unable to give an official cause of death.

On May 30th 1984, another hitchhiker on *Route 12* went missing. 17-year-old nurse *Bernice Courtemanche* vanished in New Hampshire. It wasn't until April 9th 1986, that her remains were found by a fisherman. In that instance, the cause of death was listed as knife wounds to the neck and head.

In New Hampshire on July 20th 1984, another nurse, 27-year-old *Ellen Fried*, vanished after calling her sister from a pay phone in Claremont. She spoke to her sister about a strange car that was coming and going along the road. Her own car was found abandoned the next day, just a few miles away from the pay phone. Her remains were found over a year later at a wooded area near the banks of the *Sugar River*. The coroners report confirmed she had been stabbed to death.

A year later on July 10th 1985, 27-year-old *Eva Morse* vanished after hitchhiking home from work in Charlestown, New Hampshire. A logger found her remains a year later, reports showed she had been stabbed in the neck.

On April 25th 1986, 36-year-old *Lynda Moore* was working in her yard at her home in Vermont. She was then stabbed to death during a violent struggle and was found dead later that day by her husband. Witnesses claimed they saw a suspicious man in the area and a police sketch was subsequently drawn up.

Another possible link was the April 6th 1988 stabbing of seven-months pregnant *Jane Boroski*. She had stopped her car to use a vending machine in Winchester, New Hampshire. A man was waiting at her car when she returned and accused her of hurting his own girlfriend. Boroski ran off in fear but the man stabbed her 27 times.

Miraculously she survived, crawled back to her car and drove to a friends house two miles away. She even managed to end up behind the attacker's car. Both Boroski and her child survived. Although her daughter grew up to live a relatively normal life, she was diagnosed with minor cerebral palsy due to having suffered brain damage in the attack.

As part of the investigation, Jane Boroski was put under hypnosis. She managed to describe the attack in detail. She remembered that the attacker seemed extremely calm and collected. When she stopped struggling with him, he seemed to lose interest and ceased his attack. She also described the car and partial number plate but the attacker has never been caught. After her attack, the killings stopped.

Many theories regarding the identity of the killer have been put forward in the years that followed. An Idaho police officer concluded that the police sketch was that of a convicted criminal who was in prison shortly after but nothing was confirmed.

Another suspect was *Michael Nicholaou*, a former Army helicopter pilot who served in the Vietnam War. He was accused of killing civilians in Vietnam and was discharged from the Army because of it. He claimed to have been bitter about the discharge but there are no details as to how he might have killed people in Vietnam. It is also claimed that he was responsible for the murder of his first wife but was never convicted. There is also no DNA evidence linking him to the murders.

Delbert Tallman was another suspect who confessed to killing a woman in 1984. Her murder was similar to most of the Connecticut River murders. He withdrew his confession and was found not-guilty of her murder. It is unclear why he withdrew his confession.

Gary Westover was also a suspect who confessed to being involved in the murder of Barbara Agnew; the final 1987 victim. He claimed to have abducted her with three other men and murdered her in the woods. He died shortly after the confession and no further evidence linked him to the crime.

As of 2019, the case of the Connecticut River Valley Killer remains unsolved.

Hadden Irving Clark – *The Cross-dressing Cannibal*

American murderer *Hadden Irving Clark*, AKA: *The Cross-dressing Cannibal* was suspected of being a serial killer. He is confirmed to have killed two people, one child and one adult, but it has been suggested he killed more when he confessed to killing dozens since 1974. His brother also killed a woman then dissected her, cooked her breasts and ate them.

During his childhood, he was raised by two alcoholic parents who were violent towards each other. When his mother was drunk, she referred to Clark as Kristen, and made him wear girl's clothing. His father committed suicide when he was a teenager and Clark turned to torturing and killing small animals. He also bullied other children and was generally anti-social.

He had two brothers, one of whom was *Bradfield Clark*, who was convicted of killing and cannibalising his girlfriend. His only sister ran away from home as a teenager and later proclaimed that she didn't have a family. Hadden already had a reputation for being evil. If anyone crossed him or dared to belittle him then he would kill their pets, sometimes leaving the decapitated bodies on their doorsteps. A doctor's report later divulged that Clark believed birds and squirrels spoke to him.

Hadden Clark went on to join the U.S. Navy but was discharged with paranoid schizophrenia in the same way he was fired from most of his jobs. He claimed to police later that he had been killing since 1974, when he was 22-years-old. He said he would get away with it because he was a drifter and would roam the United States, living on the streets or getting small cash-in-hand jobs.

The first confirmed murder was on May 31st 1986. He killed a six-year-old girl named *Michelle Dorr*, who was a friend of his niece, *Eliza Clark*. She had grown bored of playing alone and wandered down the street looking for Eliza, but she wasn't in. Clark then lured Dorr to an upstairs room in his brother's house – the only brother to not be in prison.

He followed her upstairs, telling her that Eliza was in her bedroom. When she stepped into the room, he pushed her to the floor and slashed her with a knife on her back before stabbing her in the throat. He attempted to have sexual contact with her corpse but instead resorted to eating parts of her body. He then squashed the corpse into a bag, cleaned up the blood, and buried the girl in a remote park nearby.

"I think I have a split personality. I don't like to hurt people but I do things I am not aware of."

Hadden Clark – quoted in a doctor's report.

Shockingly, cannibalism ran in the family. In 1984, after a night of heavy drinking and drugs, Hadden Clark's brother, Bradfield Clark, killed his short-term girlfriend *Patricia Mak*. He beat and strangled to her death then dragged the body to the bathtub. There he dissected her body, cooked her breasts on a barbecue, and ate them. He confessed to his crime and was convicted of the murder.

Six years after his first confirmed kill, Hadden Clark claimed his second confirmed kill came when he murdered 23-year-old *Laura Houghteling* in Maryland. He entered the family home dressed as a woman, then stabbed her to death while she was in her bedroom.

He suffocated her with a pillow to ensure she was dead then dragged the body to another remote wooded area and buried her body. He then returned to the house, dressed in the same women's clothes and left the house pretending to be his victim, so that people thought she was still alive if spotted.

He was caught when a fingerprint on one of her pillows matched to him. He was arrested and confessed, leading police to the body less than a year later. At the same time he led them to where he buried Michelle Dorr. He then confessed to murdering tens of women since 1974 and claimed he was the killer of the infamous *Lady of the Dunes* murder, amongst others.

"We're dealing with a serial killer here. We don't know how many people he killed. The fact is, he was a transient and moved around. How much is truth and how much of it's not? He was a very active guy for quite a long period of time. They have to see exactly what he's been up to."

Police Chief Richard Rosenthal – in a press interview for APB news.
(2000).

Clark claimed there was a body buried on his grandparents house. When police searched his grandparents property, they didn't find a body but they found a plastic tub of over 200 pieces of jewellery, including one of Laura's rings. Clark maintained that all the jewellery came from his victims.

In 1993, Clark was convicted of the murder of Laura Houghteling and sentenced to 30 years in prison. In 1999, after another trial, he was convicted of the murder of six-year-old Michelle Dorr and was sentenced to an additional 30 years in prison.

He claims to have killed many more and if the jewellery in the plastic tub is anything to go by then there might be some truth in his confessions. As of 2019, he remains incarcerated.

April 1987

April 1st

Harold Shipman, AKA*: Doctor Death,* just two days after his last victim, kills 85-year-old *Albert Cheetham* from Hyde, England. Over 80% of his victims were elderly women and he would generally ensure that he made it on to their wills before ending their lives. It was estimated that his total victim count would be over 250.

April 7th

In Texas, *Francis Elaine McLemore Newton,* shoots dead her entire family. She killed her husband, 23-year-old *Adrian Newton,* her seven-year-old son and her 21-month-old daughter.

In her trial she claimed the family were victims of a drug trade gone wrong but she was convicted of the murders and sentenced to death. On September 14th 2005, Newton was executed by lethal injection. Despite evidence against her, she pleaded innocence every day until her execution.

Lonnie David Franklin Jr. – *The Grim Sleeper*

On **April 15**[th], the body of 26-year-old *Bernita Sparks* is discovered in Gramercy Park, Los Angeles. She had died at the hands of LA-based serial killer *Lonnie David Franklin Jr.* When he was arrested in 2010 he had claimed at least 10 victims but is suspected and linked to a possible 25.

Franklin killed seven people from 1985 to 1988 but then came a 14 year gap when there were no killings. He then killed again three more times from 2002 to 2007. The gap between the killings earned him the notorious moniker of *The Grim Sleeper*.

Franklin killed over many decades and is one of the serial killer's with the longest time-span of murders. He murdered destitute black women in South Central Los Angeles over a three year period from 1985 to 1988 but resurfaced in 2002 to begin killing again.

Franklin, Jr. was a respected member of the local community and would help people to take their bins out or do some handiwork. So no one would have ever expected him to be a serial killer. In his other life as a killer of women, he would murder prostitutes, drug addicts, or homeless runaways. He generally raped them before shooting them in the chest at close range. He then left their bodies in alleyways, in trash cans, or beside industrial bins. He knew the alleys well as he was a sanitation worker at the time.

He kept his victim's underwear and jewellery as a keepsake of his crimes. When he was arrested, the investigators found a large collection of pornographic Polaroids. They depicted unconscious women, either dead or alive. There were more photographs than the killings he was convicted of, leading to speculation that he may have killed many more.

Not too much is known about his childhood but he grew up in South Central, an area of Los Angeles known for its violence and high crime rate. Police relations at the time were non-existent, and gang violence became an epidemic in the area.

However, in 1974 while in his early twenties, serving in the U.S Army as a cook, he took part in a gang-rape of a German girl whilst based in Stuttgart. He was discharged a year later due to the incident. In a 1974 trial, the victim; *Ingrid W*, explained with the help of an interpreter that Franklin and two others jumped out a car and held a knife to her throat. She was gang-raped by the three of them over the course of an entire night.

Franklin testified the encounter was consensual but was convicted in a German court where he served less than a year in prison. During the rape, Franklin was known to have taken photos of the incident, in a dark foreshadowing of the murders to come.

In 1987, he became injured while working as a sanitation worker and spent the following two decades on disability handouts. In 1988, one of his victims was *Enietra Washington*, who was 30-years-old when she accepted a ride from Franklin. He drove her to an alley, raped, beat and shot her. Washington was left for dead near some trash cans but survived. She got away alive and her testimony was instrumental in the recent court case against him.

In 2007, the *LAPD* created a task force to find *The Grim Sleeper* and this was partly due to the reporting of an *LA Weekly* journalist named

Christine Pelisek. She had noticed a pattern of murdered black women but with no reports of any arrests, so she wrote a story about it which led to the creation of the task force. It was Pelisk herself who had come up with Grim Sleeper moniker.

In 2010, Franklin was arrested after the investigation had used familial DNA searching. Franklin's son had previously been arrested for gun and drug offences, and his DNA was on the systems they searched. When they made the match, Franklin was found soon after and charged.

In June of 2016, Franklin was sentenced to death for 10 murders and one attempted murder. It has been suggested that he killed many more. He is currently on death row awaiting execution.

April 16th

Harold Shipman takes the life of 83-year-old *Alice Thomas* from Hyde, England. Shipman was convicted of 215 murders but linked to 250. Britain's health care system was modified as a result of Shipman's crimes. Arrested in 1998, he hung himself in his cell at *Wakefield Prison* in January 2004.

On the same day.

In Switzerland, serial killer *Michel Peiry, AKA: the Sadist of Romont*, claims his ninth victim, a male hitchhiker. He would abduct or lure teenage hitchhikers then tie them up and rape or abuse them. Afterwards he would violently murder them and burn the corpse.

The body was discovered in the now popular *Lake Como* region of

Italy, close to the Swiss border. He killed 11 hitchhikers between 1981 and 1987, and is said to be the worst serial killer in the country since World War Two.

April 19th

The Simpsons make their debut on *The Tracey Ullman Show*. After three seasons, the short sketches were developed into a half-hour prime time show and became *Fox Broadcasting Company's* first series to land in the top 30 ratings for a season.

The series was created by *Matt Groening* for Fox, with characters including Homer, Marge, Bart, Lisa, and Maggie. It's set in the fictional town of Springfield along with a raft of supporting characters. The series went onto become one of the most popular television shows in history and created a cultural legacy that continues to this day.

April 20th

The body of 26-year-old prostitute and drug-user *Cherie Washington* is uncovered on the property of serial killer *Morris Solomon Jr.* AKA: *The Sacramento Slayer.* Solomon had given police permission to search the car in his yard. Upon doing so they noticed a depression in the ground.

They borrowed a shovel, excavated the area themselves, and discovered Washington's body. She had been raped and killed by Solomon, before being bound, wrapped in bedding and then buried. As of 2019, Solomon is awaiting execution on death row for the murders of six women.

April 21st

In Sri Lanka, the *Colombo Central Bus Station Bombing* kills 106 people. It was a car bombing at the central bus terminal of Colombo with a 36-kilogram bomb that left a three-metre crater in the ground. The attack by the *Tamil Tigers* left 295 injured.

April 22nd

Police discover two more bodies on property owned by serial killer *Morris Solomon Jr.* AKA: *The Sacramento Slayer.* 24-year-old *Linda Vitela* and 17-year-old *Sheila Jacox* were found tied up and buried in bedding.

Both victims were prostitutes and drug-users who had been raped and murdered by Solomon. Their bodies had been in the ground for a year before being uncovered. Solomon is currently awaiting execution on death row for the murders of six women.

April 23rd

In Connecticut, the *L'Ambiance Plaza* collapses, killing 28 construction workers. The L'Ambiance Plaza was a 16-floor residential project that was under construction in Bridgeport. The half-built frame collapsed due to high concrete stresses on the foundations of the building. It was one of the worst disasters in modern Connecticut history.

April 24th

In Switzerland, eight days after his previous victim, serial killer *Michel Peiry* attacks another hitchhiker. In this instance, the man survived.

A 17-year-old man known as *Thomas*, was hitchhiking in Lausanne when Peiry picked him up. A short while after, Piery stopped the car and began attacking him. He tied him up with handcuffs, raped and beat him.

After throwing him out of his vehicle, Peiry assumed that Thomas had died but he had only pretended to be dead. Thomas ended up walking almost two miles to the village of Sottens where he was instrumental in Peiry's capture.

The *Sadist of Romont* would abduct or lure teenage hitchhikers then tie them up and rape or abuse them. Afterwards he would violently murder them and burn the corpse. He killed 11 hitchhikers between 1981 and 1987.

On the same day.

In Palm Bay, Florida, in a fit of rage, retired librarian *William Bryan Cruse* shot dead six people. He had been suffering from delusions caused by paranoia and would occasionally shoot his rifle into the air to show his distrust and hatred for people around him.

On this day in 1987, two boys accused him of making sexual gestures towards them and Cruse snapped. Later that evening, he grabbed three of his guns and went on a rampage. He killed his 14-year-old neighbour then drove to a supermarket where he killed three more people in the parking lot. He then drove to another supermarket and fired into the store at random. When police turned up, he killed two officers, one of them while the wounded officer was reloading.

He took a female hostage in the supermarket, and after a six-hour siege, he was finally captured. He left six bodies in his wake and ten people wounded. In his trial he claimed to have no memory of the attacks but in 1989 he was sentenced to death.

In 2009, while still awaiting execution, he died of natural causes at the age of 82-years-old.

April 29th

Police discover another body on property owned by serial killer *Morris Solomon Jr.* AKA*: The Sacramento Slayer.* 29-year-old *Sharon Massey* was discovered buried and wrapped in bedding near to the site of previous victim *Maria Apodaca,* who was found on March 19th 1987.

Massey had been raped and murdered by Solomon, and had been dead for approximately six months before her body was unearthed. Solomon is currently awaiting execution on death row for the murders of six women.

April 30th

The United States, under *Operation Musketeer*, carry out a 100 kiloton nuclear test at the Nevada test site, almost 2,000 metres underground. It is tested in an underground shaft and codenamed; *Hardin.*

It was either named after one of the 13 cities and towns in the United States named Hardin, or after renowned American ecologist and philosopher, *Garrett Hardin.*

Wesley Shermantine & Loren Herzog. – *The Speed Freak Killers*

The Speed Freak Killers is the moniker attributed to serial killing duo *Loren Herzog* and *Wesley Shermantine*. They were suspected to have been involved in as many as 72 murders in California from 1984 to 1999. The pair disposed of bodies in old mine shafts, remote hills, and some beneath a trailer park.

Herzog and Shermantine became friends when they were children. They were born and lived in the small town of Linden, California. They quickly became addicted to amphetamines and methamphetamine's, and made their first kill together when they were only 19-years-old.

They were arrested separately in 1999, when they were both 33-years-old. Herzog was charged with the 1998 abduction and murder of 25-year-old *Cyndi Vanderheiden*, along with four other murders dating back to 1984. It appeared that the investigation had only scratched the surface of the terror that the pair had inflicted in the region.

Shermantine was also charged with her murder. Together they were convicted of the murder of two drifter killings in 1984. 31-year-old *Paul Raymond Cavanaugh* and 35-year-old *Howard King* were found shot dead in their car on a remote area of road. Both Herzog and Shermantine would have been only 19-years-old at the time.

Herzog was also linked to and charged with the 1984 murder of 41-year-old *Henry Howell*, who had been shot dead near *Highway 88.*

Another victim was the 1985 murder of 24-year-old *Robin Armtrout*. His naked body had been discovered near a creek and he had been stabbed more than 10 times.

Shermantine was charged individually for the murder of 16-year-old *Chevelle Wheeler*. The schoolgirl had decided to skip school for the day but never returned home. DNA in her home was linked to Shermantine, but her remains are still undiscovered.

The investigation believed that Shermantine alone killed at least 20 people, with bodies scattered in old mine shafts and his own trailer park. Multiple witnesses testified against his character.

Five women came forward and stated that he had violently raped and abused them. One of them was a babysitter who had visited him to collect money that he owed her. A former wife of Shermantine claimed that he beat her for years, even while she held children in her arms.

"Listen to the heartbeats of people I've buried here. Listen to the heartbeats of families I've buried here."

Shermantine – to a woman in his trailer park.

It was their heavy amphetamine use, that birthed the moniker of the Speed Freak Killers. They killed for the thrill of killing and it was claimed that they killed for sport. Shermantine stated that he hunted humans as the ultimate thrill kill.

During the trial, both men pointed the blame at each other and implicated one another in further killings. FBI also seized over $40,000 worth of firearms from Shermantine's parents house. A large amount of technicians and forensics experts studied the weapons to see if they could link them to further murders.

In 2004, an appeals court overturned the convictions of Herzog due to the fact that his confessions were coerced. A retrial was ordered but never took place. Herzog instead pleaded guilty to manslaughter in the death of Cyndi Vanderheiden.

Herzog had his life sentence commuted to 14 years. He was paroled in 2010, causing an outcry in California. There was so much opposition that no county in the State would house him and so he was paroled to a trailer at the gates of the *High Desert State Prison* in Susanville.

In Linden, California, in February of 2010, investigators were led to a well where over 1000 bone fragments were unearthed. Shermantine had been writing letters to his sister while waiting on death row and explained where the abandoned well was. The owner of the property at the time stated that the well had been sealed up long before the murders.

It took another two years for the site to be excavated and the amount of bone fragments shocked even the hardened investigators. In March of 2012, the FBI's *Evidence Recovery Team* was drafted in to the investigation, mostly because of the way the excavation of the well was actioned.

In the same year, before more victims were found, Herzog committed suicide by hanging himself inside the trailer.

The identity of some of the remains were found to be that of two Californian teenage girls who disappeared in 1984 and 1985. Another unidentified victim was found along with the remains of a fetus. More bodies were discovered in the same year at a property owned by Shermantine's parents.

Later in 2012, Shermantine was allowed into police custody to show them four more abandoned well sites where he claimed more bodies would be found. No remains were unearthed but wild animals in the area may have consumed the bodies, had they been there in the first instance.

In 2018, the *San Joaquin County Police Department* re-opened the case of the Speed Freak Killers. In the hope that a new investigation with modern technology would link the killers to more bodies, and give families of certain missing people a greater sense of closure.

As of 2019, Shermantine is on death row at *San Quentin State Prison*.

May 1987

May 1st

Swiss serial killer *Michel Peiry*, AKA: the *Sadist of Romont*, is arrested while doing his military service in the Canton of Bern. He would abduct or lure teenage hitchhikers then tie them up and rape or abuse them. Afterwards he would violently murder them and burn the corpse. He killed 11 people between 1981 and 1987.

Peiry was raised in an unhappy home and his father was violent to both him and his mother. He grew up to lead a relatively normal life until he began to repress his homosexuality. Out of this, he leaned towards violent sexual fantasies which he acquired through a love of bondage. He claimed that sexuality and violence became inseparable.

He was sentenced to life in prison, where he remains as of 2019.

May 2nd

In South Korea, the body of 29-year-old *Park Eun-joo* is discovered. She had been tied, raped and strangled with her own clothing. She is one of ten victims of the unsolved *Hwaseong Serial Murders*. The murders took place between 1986 and 1991, and remain unsolved to this day. The killings are one of South Korea's most notorious unsolved crimes.

May 5th

In France, 10-year-old *Virginie Delmas* was abducted. Her body was discovered in October 1987, in an orchard near Paris. She had been strangled, and due to the decomposition of the body it was unclear whether she had been sexually abused beforehand.

She is suspected to have been murdered by Scottish serial killer, *Robert Black:* AKA: *Smelly Bob*. He was convicted in 1994 for the rapes and murders of four young girls in the United Kingdom. It is known he killed eight children across Europe and was suspected in 13 more. Black was a paedophile and killer who operated from 1969 to 1987. He was a truck driver who made regular work trips to mainland Europe.

The nationwide manhunt for Black was one of the most expensive and most resource-heavy UK murder investigations of the 20th Century. Robert Black remains one of the worst serial killers to walk the streets of the United Kingdom and Europe. He died of a heart attack in 2016.

May 8th

In the United Kingdom, *Harold Shipman* kills 78-year-old *Jane Frances Rostron* from Hyde, England. It was his fourth of eight victims in 1987 alone. Shipman was convicted of 215 murders but linked to 250, making him the most prolific serial killer in history by confirmed victims.

May 15th

In New York, American serial killer *Lesley Eugene Warren,* AKA: *The Babyface Killer*, raped and murdered 20-year-old *Patsy Vineyard*. Warren was a serving soldier when he met her at a bar when her husband was out of town. He took her to an abandoned barracks where he killed her and threw her body into the *Black River*.

Warren was not tried for Patsy's murder due to a lack of evidence at the time, but in 1993 he received life sentences for the brutal murders of three other women. He killed at least four women in a three year period from 1987 to 1990. Investigators suspect he was responsible for at least another eight murders of women.

As of 2019, he still remains on death row.

On the same day.

The only orbital weapons platform satellite was launched but crashed shortly after into the Pacific Ocean. The Soviet *Polyus* was a prototype weapons satellite with a mass of 80 tonnes. It was kitted out with an anti-satellite recoilless cannon, a sensor blinding laser to blind hostile satellites, and a nuclear space mine launcher. No attempt was ever made at a second launch.

May 16th

In the Soviet Union, *Andrei Chikatilo,* AKA: *The Red Ripper,* was at large. He killed three children in 1987 alone and the first was on May 16th. He lured 12-year-old *Oleg Makarenkov* with the promise of food, from a train station in the Urals town of Revda. The boy was murdered in an area of woodland close to the train station and would remain undiscovered until 1991.

The Red Ripper of the Soviet Union killed his first victim in December of 1978 and would go on to dismember and mutilate 52 people, but confessed to 56. He was sentenced to death in 1992 and executed by firing squad in 1994.

On the same day.

In California, American serial killer *Herbert James Coddington* kidnapped two teenage models and their two middle-aged female chaperones. They had fallen into Coddington's trap of pretending to hire models for an anti-drug video.

One teenage model who refused to go with Coddington gave his number plate to police which led them to Coddington's home. Two days later, on May 18th, they raided his trailer and saved the two teenage models. It was already too late for the chaperones.

The bodies of 69-year-old *Maybelle Martin* and 67-year-old *Dorothy Walsh* were discovered in an adjoining room. They had been strangled to death, tied up and hidden in garbage bags. Coddington was also charged with the 1981 rape and murder of 12-year-old *Sheila Keister* in Las Vegas.

In 1989 he was sentenced to death. His death sentence has been upheld on two separate occasions and he currently awaits execution on death row in California.

May 17th

In the Persian Gulf, the American Frigate *USS Stark* is hit with missiles fired from an Iraqi fighter jet. 37 *U.S. Navy* personnel were killed, with another 21 injured. The incident occurred during the *Iran-Iraq War*. *Saddam Hussein* claimed that the pilot mistook it for an Iranian ship, even though the *Stark* was two miles outside the exclusion zone.

May 18th

The son of infamous mobster *Jimmy Burke* was discovered in a Brooklyn street by the NYPD in the early hours. *Francis James Burke-Conway* had been shot multiple times. He was the last known suspect of the infamous *1978 Lufthansa Heist* at JFK Airport in which $5.8million USD was stolen. The heist influenced the movie *Goodfellas* in 1990.

May 20th

Ohio serial killer, *Anthony Kirkland*, murdered his 27-year-old girlfriend, *Leola Douglas*. After killing her, he set her body on fire. For her murder, he served 16 years in prison and was released in 2004.

In the five years after his release, he would go on to kill another four females. Including the aggravated murders and rapes of 14-year-old *Casonya Crawford* in 2006, and 13-year-old *Esme Kenney* in 2009, both from Cincinnati.

After various appeals and court proceedings, he was finally sentenced to death in 2018 and currently awaits his execution.

On the same day.

In Florida, 47-year-old *Audrey Gygi* is stabbed to death in her trailer in Ocean City. She was murdered by teenage American serial killer *Frank Athen Walls*. Between 1985 and 1987, Walls killed five people. He was aged between 17-years-old and 19-years-old at the time.

On July 22nd 1987, Walls slaughtered *Edward Alger Jr.* and *Ann Peterson* in their Ocean City trailer, which was near to Gygi's. For the two murders he was sentenced to death. It wasn't until 1994 while serving his sentence that he would be convicted of Gygi's murder.

As of 2019, he remains on death row awaiting execution.

On the same day.

In the United States, 'Beverly Hills Cop 2' is released. It goes on to become the second highest-grossing film in the world in 1987, behind 'Fatal Attraction'. The film rakes in $276million USD at the worldwide box office. In the United States domestic market it drops in at third place, only behind 'Fatal Attraction' and 'Three Men and a Baby'.

May 29th

In Los Angeles, 29-year-old *Carolyn Barney*, a black woman, was found dead in a vacant lot near a housing project. She was murdered by serial killer *Louis Craine*. Her body was found in the same block where Craine's parents lived.

At around the same time, a number of black serial killers were active in the Los Angeles region, and two of Louis Craine's murders were previously attributed to *The Southside Slayer*. Almost all of the victims were young black women who were either prostitutes or drug users. The bodies would be dumped in remote parks, in alleys, or in vacant buildings.

In 1989, Craine was arrested and sentenced to death for the murders of four women. He was acquitted in the trial of the fifth victim but it has since been attributed to him. Within months of being convicted he died of unknown natural causes.

Robert Black – *Smelly Bob*

In France, on **May 30**th, 10-year-old *Hemma Greedharry* was raped and strangled to death. Her body was found beside a road in a Paris suburb. She is suspected to have been murdered by Scottish serial killer, *Robert Black:* AKA*: Smelly Bob.*

He was convicted in 1994 for the rapes and murders of four young girls in the United Kingdom. It is known he killed eight children across Europe and was suspected in 13 more.

Black was a paedophile and killer who operated from 1969 to 1987. He was a truck driver who made regular work trips to mainland Europe where it is suspected he murdered dozens more. He was also prime suspect in the infamous 1978 disappearance and murder of 13-year-old *Genette Tate.* She had vanished on her newspaper delivery round in Devon, on England's Southern Coast.

Black was born in Grangemouth, Scotland, in 1947. Because his mother didn't know who the father was, she had Black adopted and he was taken in by a couple who lived in Kinlochleven, in the Scottish Highlands. He went through life with the surname of Tulip, which he took from his adopted parents. He was called 'Smelly Bobby Tulip' by school friends due to his poor hygiene – and the name stuck.

When he was growing up, he was prone to outbursts of anger and aggression and was a bully at the schools he attended. From an early age, Black believed he should have been born a girl, and at five-years-old was caught comparing his genitalia with a girl of the same age. From the age of eight-years-old, he would insert objects into his anus and carried on with the practice into his adulthood. Black was knowing to wet the bed on regular occasions, one of the many pre-cursors to violence in later life. Every time he did so, he was beaten by his foster mother and couldn't fight back, resulting in numerous and regular bruising on his body.

When he was 11-years-old, both his foster parents died from apparent natural causes and he was adopted by another couple in the small village. There, he dragged a younger girl into a public toilet and attempted to rape her. His new foster parents had him removed from their care to a mixed-sex children's care home near Falkirk on the central belt of Scotland. He abused girls there and was sent to a stricter care home for boys only. It was there that he was abused by a male carer for up to three years and would regularly be forced to perform oral sex on him.

In 1963, when he was 16-years-old, he left the care home and became a delivery boy for a local butcher's. He stated that when he delivered to houses with young girls who were alone, he would sexually assault them. He claimed to have touched or attacked at least 30 young girls on his deliveries.

In 1963, he lured a seven-year-old girl to an abandoned air-raid shelter then throttled her until she passed out, before masturbating over her body. Black was only 16-years-old at the time. He was arrested but a psychiatrists report claimed it was only a one-off and he was let go without punishment.

In 1968, he moved to London after being released from a borstal on another offence of child abuse. He moved to a bedsit near *King's Cross Station* where young children were in plentiful supply. He had multiple jobs, including a life-guard position that he was fired from for sexually touching a young girl – which comes as no surprise in hindsight.

He started collecting child pornography through a contact at an illegal book shop in King's Cross. He later managed to get hold of VHS tapes depicting child abuse. He also covertly took photos of children at swimming pools and in shops and kept the images in locked suitcases, due to the amount of material he had amassed.

He then moved into the attic of a Scottish couple in the area and got himself a long-distance driving job. In his truck he kept various disguises including different types of glasses. He also alternated between having a long beard and no beard at all.

His first confirmed murder victim was in August of 1981, when he abducted nine-year-old *Jennifer Cardy* in Northern Ireland, while on a long-haul journey. She had been riding her bike near to a main road when she vanished. Hundreds of volunteers joined the search for the girl and her body was found in a large lake, six days later by two fisherman. Black had raped and drowned the girl.

Even then, the police had suspected the killer might have been a truck driver due to the location of the lake to the trunk road. Even though it would have been someone who was familiar with the roads around it, no connection was made to Black.

His second confirmed murder victim was 11-year-old *Susan Claire Maxwell*, from Cornhill-on-Tweed, close to the Scottish border. Maxwell had been playing sports with friends before she walked home alone, before being kidnapped by Black. 300 officers and hundreds more volunteers were involved in the search and an investigation was made of every property in the area, along with a huge amount of open land.

A month later, in August of the same year, her decomposed body was found by a lorry driver in a shallow grave at the side of the road. She had been tied up and gagged, with her underwear carefully positioned under her head. Another three confirmed victims turned up from 1983 to 1987. There were also multiple disappearances and murders that were linked to Black.

In the United Kingdom alone, six disappearances and murders had been attributed to him.

8th April 1969 – 13-year-old *April Fabb* vanished while riding her bike in Norfolk. Her body was never found.

21st May 1973 – nine-year-old schoolgirl *Christine Markham* was last seen walking to school in Scunthorpe. Her body has never been found.

19th August 1978 – 13-year-old schoolgirl *Genette Tate* disappeared while delivering newspapers in the Devon town of Aylesbeare in England. Her body has never been found and the cause of her disappearance remains unsolved. It is one of Britain's most infamous and longest-running missing person inquiries. It has recently been reopened as a murder investigation by *Devon and Cornwall Police*.

28th July 1979 – 14-year-old *Suzanne Lawrence* vanished while walking from her house. Her body was never found but the location of her disappearance matched up with Blacks's route that day.

16th June 1980 – 14-year-old *Patricia Morris* vanished at the edge of her school. Her body was discovered two days later in Hounslow Heath near Heathrow. She had been strangled to death.

4th November 1981 - 16-year-old *Pamela Hastie* was found bludgeoned and strangled to death in Renfrewshire. An eyewitness put Black at the location at the time of the murder.

There were also disappearances and murders across Ireland, the Netherlands and Germany. All of the victims vanished or were killed at the same time as Black would have been in the areas on his long-haul European journeys.

In France, in 1987, a spate of child murders and disappearances have since been attributed to Black.

5th May 1987 – 10-year-old *Virginie Delmas* was abducted by Black. Her body was discovered months later in an orchard near Paris, in October of the same year. She had been strangled, and due to the decomposition of the body, it was unclear whether she had been sexually abused beforehand.

30th May 1987 – 10-year-old *Hemma Greedharry* was raped and strangled to death. Her body was found beside a road in a Paris suburb. Robert Black knew the road and area well, having made various deliveries there in the years prior to Greedharry's death.

3rd June 1987 – seven-year-old *Perrine Vigneron* vanished on her way to buy a Mother's Day card in the Bouleurs area of France. Her decomposing body was found over three weeks later. She had been raped and strangled to death in a similar fashion to the previous victim. A vehicle matching Black's truck was seen in the area around the time of the disappearance.

27th June 1987 – on the same day that the body of Perrine Vigneron was discovered, nine-year-old schoolgirl *Sabine Dumont* disappeared in Bièvres. On the following day, her body was discovered in the small area of Vauhallan. She had been raped and strangled. In 2001, Black was named as a prime suspect in her murder.

The nationwide manhunt for Robert Black was one of the most expensive and most resource-heavy UK murder investigations of the 20th century. But he was caught when a member of the public witnessed one of his abductions.

On July 14th 1990, 53-year-old retiree *David Herkes* was cutting his grass when he saw a blue van slow down on the other side of the road. Herkes started to clean the blades of his lawnmower and happened to look up to see the feet of a small girl lifting from the pavement and into the van. He watched as Black pushed the girl into the passenger seat before quickly getting in and driving away.

Already, Herkes believed he had witnessed an abduction and wrote down the registration number. He realised it might have been the six-year-old daughter of his neighbour and ran to her house where they called the police immediately. Within minutes the area was covered in police vehicles.

A short while passed and Herkes continued to describe what had happened to officers. Suddenly, Black had decided to drive back through the town on his way northwards and Herkes recognised the van instantly. He shouted to officers who jumped in front of the van and pulled Black from his seat.

The father of the missing girl, charged into the van and found his daughter tied up in a sleeping bag. She had already been sexually abused but had survived and would go on to make a full recovery. It was the last child that Black would ever touch.

He was arrested and charged. In 1994 he was convicted of the rape and murder of three girls, along with kidnapping and sexual assault. He received a sentence of life imprisonment with a minimum of 35 years. The case caused outrage in the United Kingdom and saw protests calling for the death penalty to be reinstated in the country.

Up until his death, he was charged with another murder from 1981 and was about to be charged with more when he died of a heart attack in January 2016. He was already a prime suspect in most of his suspected victims.

Robert Black remains one of the worst serial killers to walk the streets of the United Kingdom and Europe.

The Texas Killing Fields

The *Texas Killing Fields* is a 25-acre stretch of land just off *Interstate 45* that's become known as a dumping ground for the bodies of young women. Since 1971, over 30 bodies of young females aged between 12-years-old to 57-years-old have been found there. Most females are under the age of 20-years-old and had similar features.

Only a few of the murders have ever been solved, and investigators believe that most are victims of a Texan serial killer. Aside from the few murders that have been solved, the investigation carries on today. Many of the bodies found from the early 1970s to the 1980s were found to have suffered sexual assaults and were strangled but some others were not. It could have meant that multiple murderers had been using the fields to dispose of bodies.

The first known victim to be dumped in the killing fields was in 1971. 13-year-old *Colette Wilson* had disappeared from her bus stop, and her remains were discovered five months later. The coroner's report listed her death as a gunshot wound to the head.

In 1974, 12-year-old *Georgia Geer* and 14-year-old *Brooks Bracewell* vanished from their bus stop. Their classmates had previously overheard them talking about skipping school. The bodies of the two girls were discovered two years after their murder. They had been bludgeoned to death with a blunt object and then shot in the head.

In October 1983, 23-year-old cocktail waitress *Heidi Villarreal Fye*, disappeared and was presumed missing. Six months later, a dog carried her skull to a nearby house. When the rest of her remains were discovered, the coroner concluded that she had been beaten to death.

In October 1988, 22-year-old *Suzanne Rene Richerson* was abducted from the parking lot of her workplace at the *Casa Del Mar Condominiums*. One of the other employees had heard her scream and then a car door slammed shut. One of her shoes was found in the car park, but she was never seen again. Her remains were never found and her disappearance remains unsolved to this day.

One murder that was solved was that of 13-year-old *Krystal Baker* who disappeared in March of 1996. She was beaten, raped, and strangled to death then dumped at the side of the fields. Her body was found only two hours later.

In 2012, using DNA evidence found on Baker's dress, the investigation charged *Kevin Edison Smith* with the murder. Smith was already under arrest in Louisiana on a drug charge. He was spared the death penalty as investigators believed he may have killed more in the area but no positive connections were made.

In April 1997, 12-year-old *Laura Smither* disappeared from the road in front of her home in the early morning. Two weeks later, her body was discovered by a father and son out on a walk. At first they assumed it was a dead animal laying face down in a pool of water but it was the body of the 12-year-old girl. A suspect was arrested but no charges were ever brought.

As recently as April 2019, cold case investigators managed to identify two women who they believed were murdered by a serial killer, in addition to two who had been identified at an earlier date. In total, the four bodies specifically attributed to a serial killer were found between 1984 and 1991.

DNA and genetic genealogy helped them identify the women and it allowed their families to finally come to terms with their disappearances.

June 1987

June 1st

In Texas, the nude body of 41-year-old *Linda Donahew* is found in her home in Arlington. She had been raped, stabbed and strangled to death by *Roger Eugene Fain Jr.* In 2006, an Arlington cold case investigation used advancements in DNA technology to convict Fain of the killing.

He was already serving a life sentence for the 1995 murder of *Sandra Jean Dumont*, who had been killed in a similar fashion. Fain was found guilty and sentenced to a second life sentence to be served consecutively. As of 2019, he remains in prison.

On the same day.

Also in Texas, 19-year-old *Jose De La Cruz*, killed the boyfriend of his cousin, *Domingo Rosas,* who was a partially paralysed disabled man. After drinking with him for a few nights prior to the murder, De La Cruz decided to steal Rosas television. He returned with a kitchen knife and stabbed Rosas to death before stealing some of his goods and selling them for $80 USD.

De La Cruz had killed Rosas while he was still in his wheelchair and his neck had been broken in the assault. De La Cruz was captured when attempting to withdraw cash using Rosas credit card.

He was convicted of the murder and sentenced to death. On May 4th 1999, in Texas, De La Cruz was executed by lethal injection.

June 2nd

In Sri Lanka, the notorious *Aranthalawa Massacre* takes place. The *Liberation Tigers of Tamil Eelam* organization (LTTE or Tamil Tigers), killed 33 Buddhist monks, most of them young novice monks. It is considered one of the most notorious incidents committed by the Tamil Tigers during the history of the *Sri Lankan Civil War*.

June 3rd

In France, seven-year-old *Perrine Vigneron* vanished on her way to buy a Mother's Day card in the Bouleurs region of the country. Her decomposing body was found over three weeks later and it was discovered she had been raped and strangled to death.

She is suspected to have been murdered by Scottish serial killer, *Robert Black: AKA: Smelly Bob*. He was convicted in 1994 for the rapes and murders of four young girls in the United Kingdom. It is known he killed eight children across Europe and was suspected in 13 more.

Black was a paedophile and killer who operated from 1969 to 1987. Robert Black remains one of the worst serial killers to have walked the streets of the United Kingdom and Europe. He died of a heart attack in 2016.

June 18th

The United States, under *Operation Musketeer*, carries out a sub-20 kiloton nuclear test at the Nevada test site. It is tested in an underground tunnel and codenamed; *Brie.*

June 19th

In England, 16-year-old *Heather West* is raped and murdered. The date is based on DNA evidence and circumstances surrounding her disappearance, including absence from school. She was the daughter of notorious British serial killing couple, *Fred and Rosemary West.*

Her body had been dismembered with a serrated knife and later buried in a hole in their garden. An investigation into her disappearance led to the discovery of her body in 1994 and resulted in the arrest of Fred and Rose.

From 1967 to 1987, they would kill at least 12 young women. The West's turned their children and some hitchhikers into sex slaves before barbarically murdering them. They mostly buried the bodies in the garden and underneath the patio of their residence at *25 Cromwell Street;* the *House of Horrors.* Fred killed himself in prison, and Rose remains in custody serving a life sentence.

June 21st

American serial killer, *Roger Kibbe*, AKA: *The I-5 Strangler,* kills 25-year-old *Karen Finch.* He rapes and strangles her to death before dumping her body on the side of the *Interstate 5.* Kibbe killed eight young women over the course of a ten year period but it is suspected he may have killed more.

Robert Andrew Berdella Jr. – *The Kansas City Butcher*

On **June 23rd**, Kansas based serial killer *Robert Andrew Berdella Jr.* dragged a sedated 20-year-old *Larry Wayne Pearson* into his basement. He would then violently torture Pearson for the next six weeks before beheading and dissecting his remains in August of 1987. Pearson was one of six victims to fall foul of one of the most evil killers in the modern era.

Berdella was the eldest son of a deeply religious family, his father was of Italian descent. Raised in Ohio, he was sent on religious education courses and attended the local church for mass. During his childhood he was afflicted with various impediments that saw him bullied in school and beaten by his father.

When he was young, his father rarely allowed him to socialise outside of religious sermons and family chores. As such, Berdella became a loner and was known to have been socially awkward. When he was five-years-old, he was diagnosed with near-sightedness and had to wear thick-rimmed glasses. Combined with a speech-impediment, he withdrew from society at an early age.

In doing so, Berdella didn't follow in his younger brother's footsteps and take up sport, instead becoming lethargic and gaining weight. Because of this lethargy, his father would often compare him to his younger brother, belittling him for not being like his other son.

Although Berdella's father abused his children he would pay particular attention to his eldest son. He emotionally and physically abused them, sometimes beating them with a leather belt. During his school years, he was constantly bullied by other children. Teachers noted later that he was always withdrawn and lost in his own thoughts, rarely mixing with the other children. As he reached his teenage years, Berdella became confused about his sexuality, which he kept to himself. He finally came out as gay in his late teens.

On Christmas Day 1965, when Berdella was 16-years-old, his 39-year-old father died of a heart attack while at home. Berdella turned to religion in the hope that faith would somehow see him through what he described as a difficult time, regardless of his father's abuse towards him. When he didn't find what he needed, he began reading up on other religions and soon started to lose faith in what he had been taught as a youngster.

At around the same time, he had turned his withdrawal into a mask of exaggerated confidence. He became difficult to be around due to his new rudeness and attitude towards others. Then he saw a 1965 film called *The Collector*.

At the end of this chapter, we look at the influence of certain films on the minds of potential serial killers and how they might have been influenced by them. In the case of Berdella, it was one of the first known instances of a movie directly impacting the thought processes of someone who had the potential to kill *and* would go on to kill.

The plot of *The Collector* is about a man who abducts women and holds them captive in his basement. It is a direct correlation to the exact process used by Berdella in his future murders. Except that he chose men instead of women.

Two years later in 1967, Berdella moved to Kansas and went to the *Kansas City Art Institute* where he was known to have become a promising student, but things quickly took a turn for the worst. After falling in with the drug crowd, he started to abuse drugs and alcohol, and even began dealing to other students.

Some serial killers torture small animals in their childhood years, due to being able to overpower small animals where they can't overpower human abusers or carers. Berdella started late and used art as an excuse for torturing animals. As part of his art, he used sedatives on a dog to see the effects, then tortured and cooked a duck in front of other students – for art. After that he left the institute after widespread condemnation.

He was arrested a few months later in possession of Marijuana and LSD. It is unclear whether the LSD was the type known as *Orange Sunshine Acid* which is the type that Charles Manson and other known criminals went on to use. The Orange Sunshine Acid is explained in detail in *1978: Year of the Serial Killer*.

He stayed in Kansas and moved into the now infamous *4315 Charlotte Street*, in the Hyde Park area of Kansas City. He enjoyed using male prostitutes and spent a lot of time in gay bars in the city, openly taking part in casual sexual encounters with other men. He would spend time with drug addicts and homeless people and gain their trust by plying them with drugs.

Ever since his teens, he took pleasure in and saw the benefits of becoming pen-pals with people. He then wrote letters to people all over the world including to Vietnam and Burma, two countries that were very much off-limits to the Western world at the time. In return he would receive photos of ancient sites and small items from those countries, and so his collection began to grow.

In disregarding mainstream religion he had developed a belief and understanding in alternative religions and occult magic. This would lead him to opening a rather unique shop in 1982.

He opened a booth at the *Westport Flea Market* called *Bob's Bazaar Bizarre,* which was an antique and curiosity shop. It sold things like primitive art, Asian artefacts and jewellery. He subsidised his earnings by stealing items for his booth and then started taking lodgers at his home.

He became friends with the son of one of his fellow booth operators, *Jerry Howell*. When Jerry was 19-years-old, on July 5th 1984, he became Berdella's first victim.

Berdella promised to give him a lift to a dance contest but instead drugged him with heavy sedatives, took him home and tied him to his bed. Over the next 24 hours, Berdella raped, tortured and beat Jerry. He died after the drugs stopped his heart and he gagged on his own vomit. Berdella then dragged the body to the basement to try and resuscitate him but instead he suspended the body from the feet.

As Jerry's body was hanging upside down, Berdella cut his throat and other arterial veins in order to drain the blood from the corpse. A day later he returned to his basement and used a chainsaw and knives to dismember the body. He wrapped them in newspapers and put them in several trash bags, which were collected shortly after and taken to the landfill.

We know all this in such great detail because Berdella had been keeping extremely elaborate notes and photographs of his victims and other assaults. His notes detailed each individual act of torture and abuse, and outlined the intense physical and mental satisfaction that he took from carrying out the murders in such a way.

He killed another four young men after Howell and his final victim was on June 23rd 1987. *Larry Wayne Pearson* was initially one of Berdella's lodgers and Berdella hadn't planned on killing him. After he bailed Pearson out of jail, he made a crude remark about gay men, and Berdella saw red. Berdella drugged him and dragged him into the basement – where the horror began.

For the following six weeks until August 5th, when he finally killed him, Pearson was tortured and abused in the most horrific of fashions. He would be injected with drain cleaner and had piano wire tightened around his wrists to cause nerve damage. Berdella broke one of Pearson's hands with an iron bar and electrocuted him with an electric transformer.

He kept Pearson in various states of sedation and moved him around the house, including the second bedroom where he would rape and abuse him further. Towards the end, Pearson summoned the energy to bite Berdella's penis during a session of forced fellatio. Berdella then beat him to death and later dismembered him in the basement. He stored Pearson's head in the freezer before burying it in the backyard.

Although Pearson was his last murder, another victim escaped his clutches in 1988. 22-year-old *Christopher Bryson* managed to escape from the house. He jumped from a second floor window and was wearing nothing except a dog collar around his neck. He broke his foot when he jumped but managed to call out for help. Someone heard him and called the police, and Berdella was subsequently arrested.

334 Polaroid images and 34 snapshot prints were found in the apartment when it was searched. There was a possible link with a total of 20 murders but only six could be verified using his notes and confession.

Berdella was sentenced to life in prison without parole. He died of a heart failure on October 8th 1992, while incarcerated at *Missouri State Penitentiary.*

June 27th

In France, the body of seven-year-old *Perrine Vigneron*, who went missing on June 3rd, is discovered. On the very same day, nine-year-old schoolgirl *Sabine Dumont* disappeared in Bièvres. On the following morning, her body was discovered in the small area of Vauhallan. She had been raped and strangled.

She is suspected to have been murdered by Scottish serial killer, *Robert Black:* AKA: *Smelly Bob*. He was convicted in 1994 for the rapes and murders of four young girls in the United Kingdom. In 2001, Black was named as a prime suspect in the murder of Sabine Dumont.

Black was a paedophile and killer who operated from 1969 to 1987. He was a truck driver who made regular work trips to mainland Europe. Robert Black remains one of the worst serial killers to walk the streets of the United Kingdom and Europe. He died of a heart attack in 2016.

June 30th

The United States, under *Operation Musketeer*, carry out an eight kiloton nuclear test at the Nevada test site. It was exploded in an underground shaft and codenamed; *Panchuela.*

Movies that Influenced Killers

The influence of movies inspiring crime is still debated and argued over to this day. Most people who watch violent movies do not go on to re-enact what they might have seen. But there are some people that do. Before we look at some examples, let's take a closer look at the truth of it.

"Pornography and violence poison our music and movies and TV and video games. The Virginia Tech shooter, like the Columbine shooters before him, had drunk from this cesspool."

Mitt Romney, during his presidential campaign.

Romney sat on the extreme side of the fence and was in effect blaming entertainment for the reasons behind violent crime. Is the death of Simba's father in *The Lion King* any more violent than John McClane taking out bad guys in *Die Hard*?

Apparently it's only one's opinion on things that makes a difference. The assertions that violent movies cause people to become violent has been around for quite some time and a lot of research has been written on the subject. The fear has always been that watching a violent movie will make someone violent in real life. The same has always been said about gaming.

However, in an article in the *Washington Post* by *Fareed Zakaria*, he claims that people should look to Japan as a counter-argument for any claims of entertainment influencing violence. The Japanese are the biggest gaming-country in the world, when player and population ratio is looked at, yet the murder rate in Japan is close to zero. He put forward the argument that the main difference is the restrictions on firearms in Japan.

Many people want violent movies to be banned or at least restricted to a certain age group, which mostly they are. But some have claimed that it would mean censorship should reach all areas of entertainment, right down to fairy tales, which arguably have more written violence in them than most films.

On the flip-side, it has been proven that violent movies and games have more benefits than they do negatives. Researchers found that watching any type of movie, violent or not, can help people cope with their emotions. It can help people overcome challenging situations, expand their imagination, and relieve stress.

There is of course a bigger argument *against* the influence of movies on normal people. The people who go on to kill or commit crime after seeing a film were more likely to have been aggressive in the first instance. Those who commit violent crime, including murder, already exhibited aggressive traits. Such attributes were predictive of criminal behaviour, and not the viewing of movies themselves. Movies might validate one's own beliefs, rather than changing them.

The Collector (1965)

This 1965 British film is said to have directly influenced a number of cases. serial killer *Robert Andrew Berdella Jr.* AKA: *The Kansas City*

Butcher remains one of the most evil killers in the modern era. His case was one of the first known instances of a movie directly impacting the thought processes of someone who had the potential to kill *and* would go on to kill.

The plot of *The Collector* is about a man who abducts women and holds them captive in his basement to add to his *collection*. It is a direct correlation to the exact process used by Berdella in his future murders. Except that he chose men instead of women. Berdella directly cited the film as an influence of how he could kill.

The Collector was also said to have influenced the serial killing duo *Leonard Lake* and *Charles Ng*. who together in the mid-1980s killed at least 11 people but was suspected to be 25. The pair built a bunker to imprison two of their female victims. They were planning on using them as sex slaves and housemaids. They documented some of their interactions on tapes but decided to murder them instead.

They had a self-built torture-chamber in a secluded area of forest which was home to a number of elaborate torture machines on the walls and all around. They had even built a dentist's chair used for restraining their victims.

Basketball Diaries (1995)

The film featured *Leonardo DiCaprio* as a basketball player who succumbs to heroin addiction. In a dream sequence he walks into his school wearing a black trenchcoat and carrying a shotgun. Then he massacres his classmates.

The 1996 school shooting carried out by *Barry Loukaitis*, was a virtual mirror to the scene in the film. He killed three people and injured more while walking through his school wearing a black trenchcoat. He was heard quoting lines from the film. In school shootings over the years that followed, many more would wear black trenchcoats.

It is suggested that these people would have done what they did anyhow, but they used certain entertainment mediums to provide the final inspiration.

Scream (1996)

In Belgium in 2001, *Thierry Jaradin*, a 24-year-old lorry driver lured and killed his 15-year-old neighbour, *Alisson Cambier*. She had visited Jaradin's house to swap some videotapes and have a chat. She then rejected his sexual advances and he excused himself shortly after.

He returned wearing a black robe and the '*ghostface*' mask from the movie. He had two large kitchen knives in his hands as he lunged at Cambier. He stabbed her 30 times, and in doing so had ripped open the entire left side of her body. He then carried the mutilated corpse to his bed, slipped a rose into one of her hands, then called his father to confess.

In the 2006 murder of 16-year-old *Cassie Jo Stoddart*, Scream was cited yet again as a direct inspiration of the killing. After her boyfriend had left her home, two of her high school classmates went to her house and cut the power to the property. They then broke in and stabbed her at least 30 times. They had both planned the murder ahead of time and cited *Scream* and the *Columbine Massacre* as direct inspirations.

The Matrix (1999)

Unbelievably, the *'Matrix defence'* has become a real thing. The premise of the film is that our reality is not real, instead we live in a giant computer program that we only perceive to be real. Several killers used the logic that people who were killed were not real people.

In Sweden, exchange student *Vadim Mieseges* killed and dismembered his landlady. Upon his arrest he told police that he had been sucked into the Matrix. In 2002, murderer *Tonda Lynn Ansley* of Ohio, also killed her landlady by shooting her in the head. She was found not guilty by reason of insanity as she had used the Matrix defence.

Robocop 2 (1990)

American serial killer *Nathaniel White* from New York, killed six females from 1991 to 1992. He beat and stabbed them to death while on parole. White already had an aggressive personality but claimed it was *Robocop 2* that inspired him to kill his first victim.

In the film, a victim's throat was cut and the knife slit down the chest to the stomach. White copied the exact same style of murder and then left the body in the same position as it had been left in the scene of the film. He was sentenced to 150 years in prison.

Interview with the Vampire (1994)

A day after *Daniel Sterling* had watched *Interview with the Vampire* at the cinema, he took on Vampiric tendencies. *Lisa Stellwagen* had seen the film with him and visited him again the next day at his home.

He told her that he was going to kill her and savour her blood. Then he stabbed her seven times and drank her blood for several minutes. Stellwagen survived and her testimony sent Sterling to prison. Sterling later claimed that he enjoyed the movie but wouldn't blame his attack on it.

July 1987

July 1st

In Illinois, on a hot Summer evening, 10-year-old *Amy Schultz* vanishes after leaving the family home to look for a runaway dog. That night, she was raped and murdered by *Cecil S. Sutherland*.

A day later, her body was discovered in a nearby oil field. Her nude body was covered in dirt, with muddy footprints on her back, and a pool of blood around her head. After raping her, Sutherland sliced her neck from ear to ear before stamping on her body to force the blood out. Her right eye was badly damaged and her ear had been torn off.

Sutherland was arrested in October of 1987 when he began shooting at a park ranger. The DNA on Amy's body matched his and he was charged with her murder. In 1989, he was convicted and sentenced to death, which was later commuted to life without parole.

July 3rd

Virgin founder *Richard Branson,* along with his pilot *Per Lindstrand,* become the first people to cross the Atlantic in a hot-air balloon. They departed from Sugarloaf, Maine, in the United States a day earlier and arrived at Limavady, County Londonderry, in Northern Ireland on July 3rd. They covered the distance of 3,075 miles in just 31 hours and 41 minutes.

July 4th

In Aurora, in the United States, 18-year-old *Karolyn Walker* was brutally murdered by American serial killer *Vincent Darrell Groves*. Her body was found a day later. Upon his capture in 1988, Groves was suspected of killing 17 prostitutes over a 10 year period from 1978 to 1988.

This was despite being in prison on a five year term for second degree murder from 1982 to 1987. Almost immediately upon his release, he began to kill again with three bodies discovered in 1987 alone. He would eventually be convicted on two more counts of murder.

He was sentenced to life for murder. In 1996, while investigations were still continuing, Groves died in prison.

July 9th

In New York County, 12-year-old *Jennifer Schweiger* goes missing. After an intense and widespread search that lasted 35 days, her body was found in a shallow grave in a remote area of woodland. She had been raped and brutally killed.

She had been abducted by suspected American serial killer *Andre Rand, AKA: The Pied Piper of Staten Island*, who kidnapped and killed children from 1972 to 1987. It is claimed that he kidnapped them to be used in Satanic rituals but this remains unsubstantiated. He was convicted in 1987 of Schweiger's kidnapping and murder, and was sentenced to 25 years to life in prison.

Due to the *statute of limitations*, he couldn't be tried for the murder of his earlier victims and was due for release in 2008. However he was convicted on further kidnapping charges, which are not restricted by the statute. As of 2019, he remains incarcerated and is now due for paroled release in 2037.

July 10th

In Huntsville, Texas, 26-year-old *Debra Lynn Ewing* is abducted at gunpoint by American serial killer *Daniel Lee Corwin* whilst working at the *Vision Center* in the city. Her body was discovered two days later in an undeveloped plot of land. She had been raped before being strangled and stabbed.

Corwin was subsequently convicted of three 1987 murders, sentenced to death, and executed by lethal injection in December of 1988.

July 11th

In the United Kingdom, *Margaret Thatcher*, the UK's first female Prime Minister, wins a third general election with the *Conservative Party*. She wins with a majority of 101 seats and goes on to become one of the longest serving Prime Minister's in the country's history.

July 13th

American serial killer, *Samuel Little*, killed *Carol Elford* on this day. Her body was discovered on the streets of Los Angeles. DNA evidence has linked him to the murder and he is currently on trial for up to 60 more killings across the United States. He is suspected of eight murders in 1987 alone.

July 14th

In Costa Rica, we have another example of where the *statute of limitations* had passed, resulting in a serial killer getting off scot-free. Prostitute *Ligia Camacho Bermudez* was murdered in her home as she was laying on her bed reading a book. She had been shot through the window, from outside her house.

When ballistics were run, it showed the murder was carried out by a notorious Costa Rican serial killer known as *The Psychopath* (*El Psícopata*). Between 1986 and 1996, The Psychopath was responsible for the murders of at least 19 people in major cities across the country.

In 1996, the suspect was identified by the *Civil Police* but never found. Due to the Costa Rican *statute of limitations* having passed, even if a suspect was found today, he could not be tried for the murders.

On the same day.

In Spokane, Washington, coin shop owner *Leo Cashatt* was shot dead and his coin shop was robbed. He was one of the victims of *Charles Thurman Sinclair*, AKA: *The Coin Shop Killer.*

Sinclair was an armed robber, murderer and rapist of women, and was active from the early 1980s. He left a trail of bodies across Western States of America and parts of Canada. Investigators followed his crimes across the country and he was arrested in August of 1990.

He was linked to at least 11 murders and two rapes. He would specifically target coin shops to rob, before killing the owners to hide any witnesses. In October 1990, while in custody, he died of a heart attack, leaving the investigation at a standstill.

On the same day.

American serial killer, *Howard Arthur Allen,* claims his final victim. He killed elderly women between 1974 to 1987. The murder of 73-year-old *Ernestine Griffin* on July 14th, was particularly brutal and resulted in his capture.

The day before her murder, she had contacted her next door neighbour, a dentist named *Dr. Seaman.* She told him a man had stopped by her house enquiring about a car that Dr. Seaman was selling. The man had left a note with his name and phone number on.

The next morning, the dentist discovered Griffin dead in her home. She had a butcher's knife sticking out of her chest and her face had been smashed in with a toaster. A handwriting expert linked the note to Allen, which linked him to the murder. He was quickly arrested and charged.

He was sentenced to death for all three of his victims but was later commuted to 60 years due to mental incapacity at the time of the murders. He is due to be released in 2035.

July 16th

Slovakian serial killer *Juraj Luptak* is executed by hanging, after being convicted of the rapes and murders of three women between 1978 and 1982. Known as *The Strangler from Banska Bystrica*, he would hit his victims on the head with a stone and then strangle them to death.

July 22nd

In London, Palestinian cartoonist *Naji al-Ali* is shot in the head in an attempted assassination, outside the London office of the Kuwaiti newspaper, *Al Qabas*. He was rushed to hospital and remained in a coma until his death on August 27th, 1987. Multiple arrests were made, but as of 2019 the murder has never been solved.

On the same day.

In Florida, *Edward Alger Jr.* and *Ann Peterson* were slaughtered in their Ocean City trailer. They were murdered by teenage American serial killer *Frank Athen Walls*. Between 1985 and 1987, Walls killed five people. He was aged between 17-years-old and 19-years-old at the time.

He would later blame an uncontrollable rage that had grown since his childhood. For the two murders he was sentenced to death. It was while he was incarcerated in 1994 that he was linked to three more murders.

He had previously killed 47-year-old *Audrey Gygi* by stabbing her to death in her trailer in May of 1987, near to where Alger and Peterson's trailer was. He was convicted of Gygi's murder in 1994.

As of 2019, he remains on death row awaiting execution.

July 27th

Rhode Island serial killer, *Craig Chandler Price,* was arrested just before his sixteenth birthday for the murders of four women. He first killed when he was only 13-years-old on this day in 1987.

In the evening, he broke into a house only two doors away from his family home. He took a knife from the kitchen and killed the occupant; 27-year-old *Rebecca Spencer,* by stabbing her an astonishing 58 times. By the age of 15-years-old, he had killed a total of four of his neighbours, usually when high on marijuana and LSD.

His murders were so violent that the handles would break off the knives with the blades still embedded in the victims. He killed one of his neighbour's eight-year-old daughter by crushing her skull and stabbing her over 30 times.

He continues to be violent in prison, having stabbed a prison officer in 2009 and another inmate in 2017. He has never shown any remorse for his crimes and remains incarcerated for at least another 25 years.

July 29th

In the Ukrainian city of Zaporizhia, 12-year-old *Ivan Bilovetsky* becomes the thirty-sixth victim of *Andrei Chikatilo.* Bilovetsky was murdered in woodland next to a railway track. The remains were discovered by his own father a day later.

The Red Ripper of the Soviet Union would dismember and mutilate 52 people, but confessed to 56, from 1978 to 1990. He was sentenced to death in 1992 and executed by firing squad in 1994.

July 31ˢᵗ

At Mecca, Saudi Arabia, the infamous *1987 Mecca Incident* during the *Hajj Pilgramage*, was a confrontation between Shia pilgrim demonstrators and Saudi Arabian security forces. It started when the Saudi's had sealed off part of the demonstration route causing riots and stampedes. This led to 400 people being killed and over 600 injured.

Robert Pickton – *The Pig Farmer Killer*

One of Canada's worst cases of serial killing began in 1983 and continued for 19 years until 2002. *Robert Pickton, AKA: The Pig Farmer Killer,* was responsible for at least 49 murders. Even though he was only convicted on six of them. He was arrested in 2002 and charged with the deaths of another twenty women.

Forensic detection proved difficult because most of the bodies had either been decomposing for a long time or had been consumed by insects and pigs on the farm. The investigation included heavy equipment and even had 15-metre-long conveyor belts and soil sifters to find evidence of human remains.

In 2004, the *Canadian Government* confirmed that Pickton may have ground up human flesh and mixed it with pork to be sold to the public and to the wholesale trade. In conjunction with the *Health Authority*, they issued a warning about meat that had originated from the region.

Almost all of Pickton's victims were prostitutes from the Vancouver area, and in some cases it was suggested that he fed the bodies to his pigs. He was sentenced in 2010 to 25 years in prison without the possibility of parole in what was the maximum sentence for murder under Canadian law. He confessed to 49 murders but wished to kill another to make it a round fifty.

During the trial, laboratory workers confirmed that 80 unidentified DNA profiles had been detected on the evidence provided to them.

Excavations at the farm continued for a year and cost upwards of $70million CAD. The area is now fenced off and all properties belonging to the farm have now been destroyed.

Born in 1949, Robert Pickton came from a family of pig farmers based in Port Coquitlam, British Columbia, just 17 miles east of Vancouver. Pickton and his two brothers grew up on the farm and inherited it from their family. In the mid-1990s, they sold parts of the farm for a few million dollars.

A worker at the farm named *Bill Hiscox* described the remaining part of the farm as a creepy-looking place. He described Pickton as a bizarre individual who would draw attention to himself through any means possible. By 1996, Pickton had already murdered an unknown amount of victims. It was in 1996 that things took an even greater turn for the worse.

After selling off parts of the farm, the Pickton brothers neglected the farming operations and looked at events as a way to bring in money. They registered a non-profit company called the *Piggy Palace Good Times Society*. The operation involved the running and managing of events, including functions, dances, shows, and exhibitions on behalf of service and sports organisations.

Mostly it was a way to host raves and mega parties in a converted slaughterhouse on the farm, which sometimes attracted upwards of

2,000 people a night. Clientele included Hells Angels and Vancouver sex workers. The set-up provided all the victims that Pickton needed.

The raves were against the law as they would sell illegal drugs and alcohol without a license to party-goers, they also charged an entrance fee. It has been suggested that the *Piggy Palace Good Times Society* was merely a front for their illegal operations.

Pickton had been linked with missing people and murders all the way back to 1978, but was only convicted of murders that took place between 1997 and 2001. A total of 65 women had disappeared in the area from 1978 to 2001. After the largest investigation in Canadian history, investigators are still unsure as to which missing person was the first of his murders.

Prostitutes on the *Downtown Eastside* area of Vancouver were plentiful in the time that Pickton was killing. The red-light district was known for drug users, prostitutes and crime. Pickton had his pick of victims and it was reported that almost all of his victims were involved in drug use or prostitution. That a murdered prostitute is difficult to investigate, Pickton went unnoticed for two decades.

Before the illegal raves brought a raft of potential victims his way, he would lure the women to his pig farm where no one would hear them scream. He either strangled them with ligatures or shot them dead – before feeding them to the pigs.

Pigs can eat through a human body with ease, it is known that feeding a body to pigs was also used by the *Italian Mafia* at one point in their history. Because the farm processed the meat on site, Pickton had an easy method of disposal at his hands. It is also unclear whether he fed his victims to the pigs whilst they were dead or alive.

By 2001, Bill Hiscox began to notice that women would be seen entering the farm and never leaving. He finally raised his concerns to police and Pickton was arrested after women's items were found on the farm. In 2006, he pleaded not-guilty to 27 counts of murder. It is also claimed he attached a dildo to the end of his gun in order to use it as a silencer. It was then suggested that he inserted the dildo into one of the women before shooting them through it.

One of Pickton's friends, *Scott Chubb*, claimed that Pickton spoke to him about the best ways to kill hookers. He said that if she was a heroin addict then you could inject her with windscreen washer fluid. He even told Chubb that he killed prostitutes by handcuffing them and strangling them. He claimed he would bleed and gut them dry before feeding them to the pigs.

Pickton was convicted of six murders and the rest were discontinued. The court said that even if the rest were convicted then it wouldn't change the sentence Pickton had received. The difficult lack of evidence in most cases was hard to convict him on. Even though he claimed a total of 49 murders.

After his arrest, a witness named *Lynn Ellingsen* came forward to claim she had seen Pickton skinning a small woman hanging from a meat hook on his farm. She didn't tell anyone at the time as she had been blackmailing Pickton about it ever since.

In 2010, Pickton was sentenced to life with no parole for 25 years, which is the longest possible sentence under Canadian law.

David Parker Ray – *The Toy Box Killer*

From the 1950s to 1999, American serial killer and torturer *David Parker Ray*, AKA: *The Toy-Box Killer* was suspected to have killed up to 60 people. Astonishingly, no bodies have ever been found, but his accomplices statements combined with missing persons reports assured police that Ray was potentially one of America's worst serial killers.

He soundproofed and kitted out a truck trailer with instruments of torture and sexual devices, and called it his *toy box*. By the end of the trial in 2001, Ray had been convicted of kidnapping and torture but was never convicted of murder. In recent years, due to the advancements in DNA technology and investigatory procedures, he has been positively linked to 14 murders.

For the victims he raped and tortured but didn't kill, he used drugs and brainwashing techniques so the victims wouldn't remember what happened to them. The FBI later stated that the true extent of his crimes might have been stratospheric.

In the mid-1950s when he was just a teenager, he developed a fascination with bondage and BDSM. When his violent alcoholic father left him and his sister with their elderly grandfather, Ray was known to have had secret fantasies about tying people up and murdering them.

His father would supply him with pornographic magazines depicting bondage and BDSM which carved out an image of women he took into his adult years. He was also bullied by other school children for his shyness around girls. When he was in his late teens, he abducted a woman and tied her to a tree, then he tortured, mutilated, and killed her before dumping the body in the woods.

He married shortly after to a woman named *Peggy*. She claimed she knew of his fantasies but not that he was acting on them. At the time he was married, Ray became addicted to using prostitutes and took part in BDSM relationships with them.

His sole child, a daughter from the marriage, *Glenda Jean Ray*, had previously reported him to the FBI in 1986. She said that her father was kidnapping women and selling them to buyers in Mexico. The FBI didn't believe her story, saying it was too far-fetched with not enough details. It would be another 13 years before Ray was finally arrested. The FBI never commented on their mistake in not following up on the report.

The town he lived in was called *Elephant Butte* which is a small town in New Mexico. He had positioned the toy box trailer in a static location for many years, next to a large lake and area of New Mexico parkland. It has been suggested that bodies could easily be dumped in the area, due to its remoteness. But the area has never been excavated.

Ray also had extensive knowledge of the parkland, due to his position as a maintenance man for the *New Mexico Parks Department*. It is claimed that his knowledge of the land allowed him to hide bodies all over the place.

The toy box was his life's work and he spent all his earnings on it. Inside, there were detailed and intricate torture devices and machines designed to maximise pain and keep his victims restrained with minimal movement.

He would source his victims from rundown bars in the area, prostitutes, or drifters and runaways. Then he would torture his victims by using sexual instruments and industrial items. These included saws, blades, straps, clamps, whips and chains. He also had multiple accomplices, some of whom have never been named. Together they raped tens of women.

He also kept detailed illustrations regarding his various techniques for torture and restraint. He even had an electrical generator that he used to torture his victims. He would put them in large contraptions that kept them bent over in one position, and placed a mirror in front of them. Then he would bring in dogs to rape them.

Ray kept a detailed journal which contain information on his victims with dates of abductions and murders. It is claimed that without it, there wouldn't have been any prosecution. However, the FBI had built up a large case against him and three trials took place for the kidnap and torture of three victims. He was subsequently sentenced to 224 years.

In 2002, as part of his plea agreement, he agreed to show investigators where the bodies were buried. Just before he was about to, he died of a heart attack. In doing so, he took the locations of the bodies to his grave.

As of 2019, no bodies have ever been discovered.

August 1987

August 1st

In Fayetteville, North Carolina, the strangled body of 25-year-old prostitute, *Brenda Melvin*, was found in the bathtub of her room in an *Executive Motor Inn*. She is suspected to have been a victim of unknown serial killer who operated between 1987 and 1999, in the Fayetteville area.

In that time period, at least seven victims had been discovered, most of them beaten and strangled. Brenda Melvin is considered to be the first. In 1990, another victim was found strangled to death under a bridge in the same area, from then on, bodies kept piling up.

Even more chilling is the fact that many more bodies had been discovered in the area since the mid-1970s, and only recently been linked to the murders from 1987. As of 2019, most of the murders are a part of active cold case investigations. Although suspects been linked, the murders remain unsolved, and the killer remains at large.

August 4th

American serial killer *Howard Arthur Allen* is arrested in Indiana. Allen was a career criminal who killed three elderly people from 1974 to 1987, along with numerous assaults and burglaries.

He was first given the death sentence by lethal injection and spent 25 years on death row. After a long-running appeal, he was re-sentenced to 60 years on grounds of mental incapacity. He is due to be released from prison in 2035.

August 6th

In Greece, 43-year-old *Panayiotis Gaglias* was murdered by Greek serial killer *Dimitris Vakrinos*. Gaglias was a guest in Vakrino's house and had threatened to go to the police over a stolen shotgun. Vakrinos killed him as he slept in his bed by hitting him with an iron bar.

He moved the body and dumped it on the side of a highway near to his home, where it was found eight days later. Between 1987 and 1996, Vakrinos was a taxi driver who murdered five people over minor instances of disagreement. He attempted to kill another seven.

Vakrinos was caught and arrested in April 1997. In May of the same year he committed suicide in the prison's shower rooms by tying shoelaces to the shower head.

On the same day.

In Santander, Spain, 82-year-old *Margarita González* was raped and suffocated by Spanish serial killer *José Antonio Rodríguez Vega*, AKA: *The Old Lady Killer*. He forced González to swallow her own false teeth.

Vega raped and killed at least 16 elderly women from the ages of 61-years-old to 93-years-old over a nine-month period from 1987 to 1988. He was arrested in May 1988, convicted, and sentenced to 440 years in prison. In October 2002 he was stabbed to death by two other prison inmates.

August 7th

In Oregon, just before the sun rose on this day in 1987, American serial killer *Dayton Leroy Rogers* was caught red-handed in a car park. He was crouching over the mutilated body of a prostitute named *Jennifer Smith*; his seventh victim.

The witnesses jumped in their cars and chased after him, resulting in a high-speed chase across the State until Rogers somehow managed to evade capture. He was arrested at his home shortly after, where they found blood and fingerprints matching Smith's.

Rogers had become addicted to prostitutes and many came forward in his trial to claim they had been brutally raped and tortured at knifepoint. Between 1975 and 1976, Rogers raped numerous teenage girls and was sentenced for the rape of an 18-year-old girl. He was released in 1982 and continued brutalising women until he turned to murder in 1987.

Rogers killed seven confirmed victims in 1987 and was suspected of one more. Many of his victims were found with their feet cut in half or severed, probably to stop them running away. Coroner's later claimed that the injuries received by the victims were most likely carried out when they were alive. This included one who had been completely gutted.

In 1988 he was convicted of seven murders and sentenced to multiple death penalties. In 2000, the death sentences were commuted to life and he remains incarcerated in a high security prison in Oregon.

On the same day.

In the Bering Strait, *Lynne Cox* becomes the first person to swim between the United States and the Soviet Union, in a feat that both country's leaders claimed eased Cold War tensions.

She swam in freezing temperatures from the island of Little Diomede in Alaska, to Big Diomede in the Soviet Union. At the time, because of the Cold War, the Inuit communities on both islands were not allowed to travel to the other.

On December 8th, 1987, *President Reagan* and last leader of the Soviet Union, *Mikhail Gorbachev*, signed an arms treaty at the White House. Gorbachev gave a speech where he cited Lynne Cox as an inspiration to both countries.

"Last summer it took one brave American by the name of Lynne Cox just two hours to swim from one of our countries to the other. We saw on television how sincere and friendly the meeting was between our people and the Americans when she stepped onto the Soviet shore. She proved by her courage how close to each other our peoples live."

Mikhail Gorbachev at the White House in December of 1987.

August 8th

The body of Irishman *Trevor O'Keeffe* was discovered in a shallow grave in France. He had been hitchhiking through the country when he was strangled to death by French serial killer *Pierre Chanal*, who had operated in the *'Triangle of Death'*. Seven young men had disappeared within the triangle since 1980.

In 1988, Chanal was stopped by police. When they opened his van doors, they discovered a Hungarian hitchhiker who had been tied and gagged. He was convicted of kidnapping and rape. Chanal was suspected to have killed between eight and 17 people in the Mourmelon region of France between 1980 and 1988.

His van was full of sex toys and a camera where he had been taking various images of men he had picked up. Unbelievably, Chanal was a *Chief Warrant Officer* in the *4th Dragoon Regiment* in France. He had previously earned a United Nations medal for his service as a UN peacekeeper in Lebanon.

Pierre Chanal committed suicide in 2003 whilst on trial for the murders.

August 9th

In Australia, *The Hoddle Street Massacre* takes place in Melbourne, sometimes known as the *Clifton Hill Massacre*. An Australian Army Officer cadet, 19-year-old *Julian Knight,* killed seven people and injured 19 others.

After a police chase, Knight was finally caught and sentenced to seven consecutive life sentences. He has never offered any motive for the mass-shooting and remains incarcerated at the maximum security

Port Phillip Prison in Victoria. The incident has been the source for various books and documentaries.

The mass shooting was not the only one in Melbourne in 1987. On December 8th, *The Queen Street Massacre* was carried out by half-Croatian, half-Italian *Frank Vitkovic*. He entered the *Australia Post Offices* in Melbourne, carrying a sawn-off semi-automatic carbine gun in a brown paper bag. He strolled up to the fifth floor and began firing into the office, killing nine people and leaving five injured.

August 13th

In Northern Carolina, 73-year-old *Ruth Constantine* was beaten to death in her home as she was being robbed. She had been killed by *The Day Stalker* who was known to have been *Franklin Lynch*.

He was arrested in October 1987, and charged with three murders. In 1992, Lynch was sentenced to death for Constantine's murder. He was linked to at least 10 more murders within the region during 1987 but a lack of evidence has made prosecutions difficult. In 2010, an appeal against his death sentence was rejected.

As of 2019, he remains on death row, to the detriment of the families of his victims.

On the same day.

The United States, under *Operation Musketeer*, carry out an 150 kiloton nuclear test at the Nevada test site. It is tested in an underground shaft and codenamed; *Tahoka*, which is a city in Texas.

August 15th

When he was just 16-years-old, *Clinton Bankston Jr.*, hacked to death three women. 63-year-old *Ann Morris*, 59-year-old *Sally Nicholson* and 22-year-old *Helen Nicholson* were slaughtered with a hatchet. The bodies were so badly mutilated that they could only be identified in post-mortem.

When he was arrested the following day, it emerged that Bankston had murdered two more people back in April of 1987. Bankston then created a pseudonym under the name of *Chris*, claiming that Chris had taken over his body during the murders.

A year later in 1988, when he was 17-years-old, Bankston was convicted of five murders and sentenced to five life sentences. He was only saved from the death sentence due to his age.

As of 2019, he remains incarcerated.

August 17th

In Pennsylvania, American serial killer *Harrison Graham* is captured. He had been wanted for the 1986 murders of seven women in Philadelphia between the ages of 22-years-old and 36-years-old. He would kill them while he was under the influence of drugs and mostly at the same time as having sex with the victims.

He kept the bodies of his victims in his apartment, wrapping them in bedding and piling them up in his bedroom. The bodies were found after an eviction notice was served due to bad smells coming from the apartment. He turned himself in after a week on the run after his mother convinced him to.

He was convicted of seven murders and sentenced to death which was later commuted to life after an appeal regarding his mental health. As of 2019, he resides at the *State Correctional Institution Coal Township* (SCI Coal Township) in Pennsylvania.

August 19th

In England, *The Hungerford massacre* leaves 16 people dead in a spree of random shootings. *Michael Robert Ryan* was a jobless antique dealer and handyman, who carried out the shootings using a handgun and two semi-automatic rifles.

He shot people at a school he had once attended and at several other locations around Hungerford before turning the gun on himself. No motive was ever recorded. It remains one of the deadliest firearm-related incidents in the country.

August 28th

Three different convicted murderers, in three different American States, were executed at the same time on this day in 1987.

In Utah, *Pierre Dale Selby* was executed. In 1974, two U.S. Air Force Airmen, Selby and *William Andrews* robbed a Hi-Fi shop and killed three hostages. They also raped and mutilated their victims. The case became known as the *Hi-Fi Murders*. Andrews was executed in 1992.

On the same day.

In Alabama, *Wayne Eugene Ritter* was executed. In 1977, Ritter and an accomplice went on a robbery spree that left one person dead. The spree also involved 30 armed robberies and nine kidnappings. Although it was Ritter's accomplice that shot dead a pawn shop owner, they were both sentenced to death for their crimes. In 1983, his accomplice, *John Louis Evans III*, was executed in the electric chair.

On the same day.

In Florida, *Beauford White* was executed. In 1977, he shot and killed six people and wounded two others during a robbery and raid on a drug dealer's home in Miami. White was executed in the electric chair. His accomplice, *Marvin Francois*, was executed in the same manner in 1985.

August 31st

American serial killer *Billy Richard Glaze, AKA: Jesse Sitting Crow*, was arrested on this day. Glaze was a suspect in the murders of three Native American women in the Minneapolis area at the time and was caught while driving under the influence of alcohol. The arresting officers found a bloody shirt and a crowbar in the car.

Evidence in hair samples taken from the crowbar were used to convict him of the three murders. Glaze was suspected of involvement in a possible 50 murders, but with the evolution of DNA technology, Glaze's guilt has been brought into question. It is suspected now that he had no involvement in the crimes, as DNA evidence points to an unknown male in the murders. A new investigation is currently open and active.

In 2015, Glaze died of lung cancer in prison, after spending 25 years inside.

On the same day.

While serial killer *Dayton Leroy Rogers* was under arrest for an August 7th, murder, another one of his victims was discovered. A 46-year-old crossbow hunter named *Everett Banyard*, came across the partially clothed decomposed body of a young female.

Over the following week, authorities unearthed six more decomposed corpses, all within a small circle of Molalla Forest. The murders became known as *The Molalla Forest Murders* and one of the worst serial killings in the history of Oregon. Rogers killed seven confirmed victims in 1987 and was suspected of one more.

Most victims had their feet removed or cut in half and one woman had been gutted. In 1988 he was convicted of seven murders and sentenced to multiple death penalties. In 2000, the death sentences were commuted to life and he remains incarcerated in a high security prison in Oregon.

On the same day.

International pop star, *Michael Jackson*, releases *Bad*, his third solo album. At the time it became the second best-selling album in history, behind Jackson's previous release; *Thriller*.

Project E-Pana – *Highway of Tears*

Project E-PANA was created in 2005 to review and investigate numerous unsolved murders on *Highway 16*, which became known as the *Highway of Tears*. The investigators chose the name of PANA as it is an Inuit word describing the spirit goddess who looks after souls before they go to heaven.

The task force was set up by the *Royal Canadian Mounted Police* (RCMP) with the exclusive purpose of solving cases of missing and murdered people along the Highway. Highway 16 runs between Prince Rupert and Prince George, two cities in British Columbia that are 446 miles (718 km) apart. After just one year from the formation of the project, the investigation expanded to include Highways 5, 24 and 97.

In 2006, the task force had nine active investigations on the books. A year later in 2007 they had doubled to eighteen. The cases being investigated were cold cases from 1969 to 2006 and because more murders were diluting the investigation, they created a specific set of rules. These rules allowed them to focus on specific cases in the region and meant they could be added to the project E-PANA list.

- Victims had to be female.

- Involved in hitchhiking or prostitution, or other high-risk behaviours.

- Last known location to be within a mile of the three major British Columbia highways; 5, 16 and 97. This could have been the last time she was seen alive or where her body had been found.

- Cases where evidence pointed to a stranger having committed the crime rather than a domestic attack or accident.

The murder victim list.

- October **1969** – 26-year-old *Gloria Moody* – Last seen leaving a bar in Williams Lake. Her body was found in the woods at a cattle ranch six miles away.

- July **1973** – 18-year-old *Micheline Pare* – Last seen beside the gates of Tompkins Ranch near Hudson's Hope. Two women had previously dropped her off there. Her body was found in the area in August 1973.

- October **1973** – 19-year-old *Gale Weys* – She vanished while hitchhiking from Clearwater to Kamloops. Body was found in a ditch on *Highway 5* just south of Clearwater. Suggested to have been a victim of serial killer *Bobby Jack Fowler*.

- November **1973** – 19-year-old *Pamela Darlington* – Vanished from Kamloops while hitchhiking to a local bar. Her body was found the next day. Suggested to have been a victim of serial killer *Bobby Jack Fowler*.

- December **1974** – 14-year-old *Monica Ignas* – last seen walking home alone from school. Her remains were found in April 1975, hidden in a dense forest. She had been strangled to death.

- August **1974** – 16-year-old *Colleen MacMillen* – her body was discovered in September 1974. She was last seen leaving her home to hitchhike to a nearby friend's house. DNA evidence matched *Bobby Jack Fowler* to the murder who was also working in the area at the time.

- May **1978** – 12-year-old *Monica Jack* – In one of the more well known crimes in the area, Monica was last seen riding her bike near her home. Her disappearance remained a mystery until her skeletal remains were found by forestry workers in 1995. Serial murderer *Garry Taylor Handlen* was charged with her death along with another 11-year-old girl. On January 18th 2019, Handlen was finally convicted.

- May **1981** – 33-year-old *Maureen Mosie* – She had been hitchhiking from Salmon Arm to Kamloops when she disappeared. Her body was found the next day by a woman walking her dog. She had been beaten to death.

- August **1989** – 24-year-old *Alberta Williams* – Her body was discovered a month later, just over 20 miles east of Prince Rupert. She had been raped and strangled to death.

- June **1994** – 16-year-old *Ramona Wilson* – She was hitchhiking from Smithers to stay with friends in Hazelton but she vanished. Her remains were discovered in April 1995 near the Smithers Airport. Several items were in a small organized pile a few feet away from her, these included a section of rope, three interlocking ties and a small pink water pistol.

- July **1994** – 15-year-old *Roxanne Thiara* – A prostitute who went missing in Prince George. She told her friend she was going off with a customer and she was never heard of again. Her body was found a month later in a bush along Highway 16. She was friends with the next victim on the list.

- December **1994** – 15-year-old *Alishia Germaine* – Her body was found behind an elementary school outside of Prince George, just off Highway 16. She had been stabbed to death and was friends with Roxanne Thiara who had been killed a few months earlier. They had been seen working together multiple times before their deaths.

- February **2006** – 14-year-old *Aielah Saric Auger* – Her body was discovered in a ditch on Highway 16, just a few days after she went missing.

The missing persons list.

- **1983** – 17-year-old *Shelley-Anne Bascu* – Vanished in 1983 and her body has never been discovered. However, personal items such as clothing and blood matching her blood type were found beside the Athabasca River. She is still officially a missing persons case.

- June **1990** – 16-year-old *Delphine Nikal* – She had been hitchhiking from Smithers in an Easterly direction when she vanished. The teenager's body has never been discovered and she is a missing persons case to this day.

- October **1995** – 19-year-old *Lana Derrick* – She was last spotted getting into a car with two unidentified men, at a service station in Thornhill. She has been missing ever since and no sign of a body has ever been found.

- June **2002** – 24-year-old *Nicole Hoar* – in a similar fashion to the others, she was last seen hitchhiking to Smithers. She had been spotted at a service station just west of Prince George. An investigation suspected convicted murderer *Leland Vincent Switzer.* A search was carried out on his property but they found no sign of any human remains. Hoar has been missing ever since.

- September **2005** – 22-year-old *Tamara Chipman* – She was last seen in Prince Rupert and had been hitchhiking east on Highway 16. As of 2019, no sign of her has ever been found and she remains a missing person.

As of 2019, only one murder has been solved and that was the infamous death of 12-year-old *Monica Jack*. Serial murderer, *Garry Taylor Handlen* was charged with her murder and the death of another 11-year-old girl.

American serial killer *Bobby Jack Fowler* was linked with DNA evidence to the murder of 16-year-old Colleen MacMillen. Fowler had also been working in the area at the time. He has also been linked with a number of other E-Pana investigations and is the prime suspect in the murders of Gale Weys and Pamela Darlington.

In 2012, they used the advancement in DNA technology to positively identify him in the murder of MacMillen. The Royal Canadian Mounted Police strongly believe that he was responsible for at least 10 of the other victims on the list. However, many more murders took place after his arrest in 1995, when he was picked up on a rape charge.

As Fowler died in prison in 2006, the investigation of his suspected murders has been made more difficult. Since 2010, the E-Pana investigation has lost 58 officers, dropping from 70 at its peak, to just 12. This has been due to budget cuts for the E-Pana caseloads.

As of 2019, all cases are still active.

September 1987

September 3rd

American serial killer *Samuel Little*, killed *Guadalupe Apodaca* on this day. Her body was discovered on the streets of Los Angeles. DNA evidence has linked him to the murder and he is currently on trial for up to 60 more killings across the United States.

Samuel Little was in a homeless shelter in Kentucky when he was arrested in 2012 following DNA testing on various cold cases. He could be America's most prolific serial killer but as of 2019, the trial is still ongoing.

September 11th

In England, retired architect *Simon Dale* was found bludgeoned to death in his countryside mansion, *Heath House*, in Shropshire. He died either on September 11th or 12th, the disparity is due to not being able to pinpoint the exact hour of death. His body was left in a pool of blood beside an open cooker which confused the rigor mortis process.

His ex-wife, *Baroness Susan de Stempel*, was cleared of his murder due to insufficient physical evidence but was subsequently charged with fraud. The murder of Simon Dale has never been solved but the story persists to this day.

Other elements to the story include Hollywood actors, properties in Monaco, a previous murder at Heath House, and a possible link to £12million GBP worth of gold bars that may or may not still be buried in the grounds.

September 14th

In the United Kingdom, *Harold Shipman* kills 71-year-old *Nancy Anne Brassington*. It was his fifth of eight victims in 1987 alone. Shipman, also known as *Doctor Death*, was convicted of 215 murders but linked to 250. He is the most prolific serial killer in history by confirmed victims.

September 15th

In Leningrad, 16-year-old school student, *Yuri Tereshonok*, was lured off a train and murdered by *Andrei Chikatilo*. After his arrest, he led investigators to the site of the remains. *The Red Ripper* dismembered and mutilated 52 people from 1978 to 1990.

On the same day.

In Michigan, 15-year-old *Randy Laufer* vanishes, he was murdered by serial killer and paedophile *John Rodney McRae*, who killed up to five young boys between 1950 and 1997.

Back in 1950, when McRae was only 16-years-old, he killed his eight-year-old neighbour and was subsequently sentenced to life in prison to be paroled in 1972. Up until his second arrest in 1998, many children had gone missing that would soon be linked to him.

Laufer's bones were discovered on McRae's former Michigan property in 1997 and McRae was arrested shortly after. In 1998, he was sentenced to life for the Laufer murder but is suspected to have been involved in the disappearance of at least five boys in total.

In 2005, McRae died in prison of natural causes.

Roger Kibbe – *The I-5 Strangler*

On **September 17**[th], American serial killer *Roger Reece Kibbe* kills 17-year-old runaway and prostitute *Darcie Frackenpohl*. He strangled her to death after raping and beating her. He went on to remove her hair and then dumped her body near Echo Summit in California.

Darcie was Kibbe's final known victim as most of his murders took place in 1986. Most of the bodies were dumped on the side of the *Interstate 5 (I-5)*, one of the longest road systems in the United States. Police discovered abandoned cars on the highway that belonged to some of the victims. At the time it was suspected that Kibbe patrolled the area searching out females with broken-down cars.

Very much murders of the time which harks back to the notion that the highways opened up *killing channels* for serial killers to move back forth between states.

Roger Kibbe was born in 1949 to a violent mother who regularly beat him. He spoke with a stutter and was bullied by other children in school because of it. He developed an unhealthy view of women in his teenage years, most likely caused by the abuse he had received.

In his teenage years he was arrested for stealing women's underwear from clotheslines. Unknown to the police at the time, Kibbe took pleasure in tying himself up with the underwear and taking sexual satisfaction in doing so. He would always cut up the items he stole with a pair of his mother's scissors, something that would be his modus operandi in years to come.

He married in his adult years to a dominant woman that reminded him of his mother, but not too much is known about that particular relationship.

Roger Kibbe's brother was a homicide detective and so it was suspected that he used his brother's knowledge about crime scenes to hide his true identity from any investigation that ensued. He learned how investigators would approach cases similar to his own murders. Because of this, no fingerprints or semen was found on his victims.

His first victim was in September of 1977, when he put a fake job advertisement in a business school. The job was for a secretary at a fake cosmetics studio. He did it with the sole purpose of finding a young female to rape and murder. 21-year-old student *Lou Ellen Burleigh* responded to the advertisement. Kibbe told her that his office was under construction and to meet in his van where he drove her to Lake Berryessa in Napa County.

He raped and strangled her before dumping her body near a riverbed. It would take 34 years for Burleigh's remains to be found. In 2011, a small bone was found in the area and DNA results confirmed it had belonged to her. Kibbe wouldn't kill again until April 1986, when he would kill five people in the same year.

He killed *Karen Finch* on June 21st 1987, before the September 1987 slaying of Darcie Frackenpohl. And it was Frackenpohl's murder that would lead to his arrest and conviction. Her body was discovered by a jogger two weeks after she was killed.

After abducting, raping and strangling his victims he would proceed to cut open their clothes in irregular shapes with his mother's scissors. It was never clear why he did this but it stemmed back to his childhood fascination of cutting up the underwear he had stolen.

It has been proposed he did this to mentally cleanse himself of the crime. Another suggestion is that he touched the person in those areas and cut the clothing away to hide the evidence. Although this seems unlikely as it would have been easier to remove the clothing entirely, thus a deeper psychological reason must have been prevalent. He also removed the hair of some of his victims to remove the duct tape he had bound them with.

In April 1988, Kibbe was arrested and went to trial later in the year for Darcie's murder. At the time there was insufficient evidence to link him to the other murders, even though police were sure he was the I-5 Strangler. In March of 1991 he was finally convicted of Darcie's murder and sentenced to 25 years.

When DNA technology advanced enough, further charges were brought to Kibbe and he made a plea bargain in 2009 to avoid the death penalty. He received six additional life sentences for the murders and remains incarcerated at *Mule Creek State Prison* in California. He is known to have killed eight people but has been linked to numerous more.

September 18th

In Virginia, 35-year-old account executive *Debbie Dudley Davis*, was murdered in her apartment by serial killer *Timothy Wilson Spencer*, AKA: *The Southside Strangler*. Her naked body was discovered the following day when she failed to appear for work. She had been raped and strangled to death.

Spencer killed five people, one in 1984, and four in 1987, but is suspected of others. A copycat killer killed another in 1988, a murder which was initially attributed to *The Southside Strangler*.

Spencer is known for being the first serial killer in the United States to be convicted on DNA evidence. For the murder in 1984, another man named *David Vasquez* was wrongfully convicted, and he became the first person to be freed because of DNA evidence.

On the same day.

In the United States, the *Michael Douglas* and *Glenn Close* thriller, *'Fatal Attraction'* is released. It goes on to become the biggest film in the world in 1987, taking in $320million USD at the worldwide box office. In the United States domestic market it is the second highest grossing film behind *'Three Men and a Baby'*.

September 19th

In Richmond, Virginia, *Debbie Davis*, was found dead in her first floor apartment that she lived in alone. She had been strangled with a sock that had been tied around her neck, then twisted tight with a small section of pipe.

She had been raped and strangled by serial killer *Timothy Wilson Spencer,* AKA: *The Southside Strangler.* Spencer would be convicted of five murders from 1984 to 1987, and was the first serial killer in the United States to be convicted on DNA evidence.

September 22nd

In Isle of Wight County, Virginia, 20-year-old *David Knobling* and 14-year-old *Robin Edwards* were found shot to death. The dating couple were discovered in the *Ragged Island Wildlife Refuge*, on the south shore of the James River. The two bodies were found by Knobling's father and a search party who were scouring the edges of the river.

They are claimed to be victims of an unidentified serial killer who killed at least eight people along the Colonial Parkway area of the U.S. Commonwealth of Virginia. In a three year period from 1986 until 1989, three couples were murdered and one couple went missing, presumed dead.

Collectively, the murders became known as *The Colonial Parkway Murders* and remain unsolved to this day.

September 24th

The United States, under *Operation Musketeer*, carry out a 150 kiloton nuclear test at the Nevada test site. It is exploded in an underground shaft and codenamed; *Lockney*, which is a town in Texas.

September 25th

In Missouri, 40-year-old *James Schnick* shot dead seven of his family members in a bizarre attempt to claim money from their wills and life insurance. He even shot himself and planted the gun on his 14-year-old nephew to incriminate him.

It didn't work. In 1992, he was convicted and sentenced to death which was later commuted to three life sentences without the possibility of parole. As of 2019, he remains incarcerated.

September 30th

In Santander, Spain, 80-year-old *Carmen González Fernández* was found dead in her home. She had been raped and murdered by Spanish serial killer *José Antonio Rodríguez*, AKA: *The Old Lady Killer*.

He generally identified a victim before watching her every move, learning every detail of the routine. Then he would make contact in an attempt to gain her trust until he was invited into her home, whereupon he would kill them. It has been suggested that he killed elderly women due to an extreme hatred of his mother.

Rodríguez raped and killed at least 16 elderly women from 1987 to 1988. He was arrested in May 1988, convicted and sentenced to 440 years in prison. In October 2002 he was stabbed to death by two other prison inmates.

The Colonial Parkway Murders

Between 1986 and 1989, an unidentified serial killer was suspected of killing at least eight people along or nearby the Colonial Parkway of the United States Commonwealth of Virginia. Three couples were murdered and one couple went missing. It has also been suggested that another two people may have fallen victim to the same killer.

In most countries, the construction of highways or motorways was one of the reasons why serial killing increased through the 1970s and reached a peak in the 1980s. Life was also made extremely difficult for law enforcement because of various State boundaries that existed.

It also meant that a serial killer's potential victim might not be recognised as such due to the then disconnected reporting between authorities. The highways provided an opportunity where there wasn't one before. The killings in this three year period were referred to as *The Colonial Parkway Murders*.

The first recorded murders took place on October 9th, 1986. 21-year-old student *Rebecca Ann Dowski* and 27-year-old *Cathleen Marian Thomas* disappeared while out together. It wasn't until October that a jogger spotted a white car alongside the York River. Inside the car, both Thomas and Dowski were found, they had been strangled and mutilated.

A coroner's report confirmed they had been tied with rope, strangled and then had their throats slit. Gasoline had been poured on the bodies to hide evidence but the killer or killers had been unable to light it. Their belongings were found in the car meaning that it hadn't been a robbery. Since the murders took place on federal property, the case fell under FBI jurisdiction. Over 150 fingerprints were found but did not match any person on the FBI database.

On September 22nd 1987, in Isle of Wight County, Virginia, 20-year-old *David Knobling* and 14-year-old *Robin Edwards* were found shot to death. The dating couple were discovered in the *Ragged Island Wildlife Refuge*, on the south shore of the James River. The two bodies were found by Knobling's father and a search party who were scouring the edges of the river.

According to those who knew them, Robin Edwards was an older-looking 14-year-old and had been known for dating older men. However, if the relationship was a sexual one then it would have been illegal under the laws at the time. No shell casings were found and some believe a revolver could have been the murder weapon. Since the Ragged Island Wildlife Refuge was state property, then the case was taken over by the State Police and not the FBI.

On April 9th 1988, 18-year-old *Cassandra Lee Hailey* and 20-year-old *Richard Keith Call* went missing. Richard's abandoned vehicle was found on the Colonial Parkway, only three miles from where the bodies of the two previous victims were discovered. The keys were still in the ignition and the driver's side door was left open.

As of 2019, their disappearance has never been solved but it has been suggested they may have been murdered, as all the clothes they were wearing when they had gone missing were found inside the car. The case fell under FBI jurisdiction. The family said the car must have been positioned in its resting place as the couple had never used that section of road.

On September 5th 1989, 18-year-old *Annamaria Phelps* and 21-year-old *Daniel Lauer* disappeared. At the time of the disappearance, Annamaria had been dating Daniel's brother and was assumed to be having an affair with Daniel. Their bodies were found by deer hunters in the area on October 19th 1989, at a secluded logging road.

The area they were found in was 30 miles away from the I-64 ramp onto Colonial Parkway. The two deer hunters had come across a blanket in the woods, when they lifted it up they found the skeletal remains. Although cause of death could not be determined, knife marks were found on the bones of Annamaria.

There were two more murders that may have been connected with the Colonial Parkway murders. In 1996, 24-year-old *Julie Williams* and 26-year-old *Lollie Winans*, who were a young couple, were backpacking through the *Shenandoah National Park* with their Golden Retriever. They set up camp just a few feet away from a horse trail. They were last seen by a Park Ranger who renewed the camping permit and dropped them off at the *Stony Man* car park.

When they were reported missing, park rangers found their car and the dog, who was roaming the area. They then found both bodies nearby. They had been bound and gagged with duct tape and were half-naked, their throats had been cut so deeply that they were virtually decapitated. It has never been clear whether these two murders were the work of the same killer who was operating in the mid to late 1980s, but it hasn't been ruled out.

In 2010, *Detective Steve Spingola* released a document regarding the murders and claimed they were possibly killed by different people. He claimed that the Thomas and Dowski murder could be connected to the Shenandoah murders of Lollie Winans and Julie Williams. He theorized that the two double murders could have been the work of a serial killer targeting lesbian couples.

Some other investigators believe that the killings might have been committed by someone who worked in law enforcement. The windows on the cars were all wound down, leading one investigator to suggest that the only reason to have done so was if they were being pulled over by an officer or ranger.

A deputy who was around at the time, named *Fred Atwell*, has constantly been mentioned as a person of interest. Most families of the victims stated that his obsession with the murders was unhealthy, and he worked his way into their lives, too intimately to just be friendly. He was arrested in 2011 for robbing a woman at gunpoint.

As of 2019, The Colonial Parkway Murders have not been solved and remain a cold case investigation to this day.

October 1987

October 1st

In South Africa, the seventh victim of South African serial killer *Norman Simons* is discovered, almost a year to the day of the discovery of the first victim. The unnamed boy was also found in exactly the same location as Simons very first victim, at *Modderdam Railway Station*, near Cape Town.

He was one of 22 victims of Simons, who was active between 1986 and 1994. The unnamed boy had been raped and strangled to death with a piece of his own clothing. Norman Simons is considered to be one of South Africa's worst known serial killers.

October 2nd

Dr. Susan Hellams, a resident in neurosurgery at the *Medical College of Virginia* in Richmond, was raped and killed in her home. She was murdered in her apartment by serial killer *Timothy Wilson Spencer*, AKA: *The Southside Strangler*.

Her body was found by her husband in the early hours of the following morning. She had been strangled by two belts which were found around her neck. Spencer would be convicted of five murders from 1984 to 1987. He was the first serial killer in the United States to be convicted on DNA evidence.

October 6th

In Fort Worth, Texas, an unnamed woman awoke in the middle of a sexual attack from American serial killer *Juan Segundo*. He carried on the attack and then physically assaulted her before fleeing the property.

The unnamed victim survived the ordeal but at least four others died at the hands of Segundo. He was sentenced for the burglary of the house to ten years in prison but was released only one year later. It wasn't until 2005, when a cold case investigation linked DNA to him, that he was arrested for murder.

He was sentenced to death for the 1986 rape and murder of 11-year-old *Vanessa Villa*, who he strangled to death. He was also linked by DNA evidence to three more murders between 1994 and 1995. Segundo is currently on death row awaiting execution by lethal injection.

October 10th

In Australia, mass murderer *John Tran* killed his ex-fiancee and four members of her family by shooting them dead. He had been engaged to *Lieu Huynh* until a month earlier, when she broke it off and became engaged to another man.

Tran turned up at her family's house and shot dead her father first before rampaging through the home and shooting dead her mother, sister and one brother. He found Lieu in the garden and killed her with a single shot before shooting himself in the head.

October 11th

In Scotland, a 24-boat flotilla packed with sonar equipment end their search for the *Loch Ness Monster*. The major million-dollar *Operation Deepscan* spent a week on the loch and failed to find any evidence of the supposed monster. Still to this day there are sightings of the monster, usually from local people who own businesses – beside the loch.

October 12th

In Vancouver, *Vanessa Lee Buckner's* body was found naked on the floor of the *Niagara Hotel*. She was murdered by Canadian serial killer, *Gilbert Paul Jordan*, AKA: *The Boozing Barber*, who would use alcohol as a weapon. Buckner's death was caused by Jordan supplying her with a fatal level of alcohol.

Jordan was linked to the murders of up to ten women over a 22 year period and used alcohol as a murder weapon. His other convictions were for rape, assault, kidnapping, hit and run and car theft.

He would seek women in bars and ply them with drink, sometimes paying them for sex. Because some of his victims were alcoholics, the police paid little attention. He was known to have drunk almost two bottles of vodka every day.

October 13th

In Indiana, American serial killer *Michael Lee Lockhart* killed 16-year-old *Wendy Gallagher*. He raped and mutilated her before stabbing her to death. Her body was discovered in the bedroom of her family home by her sister. She was partially clothed with her hands tied behind her back.

She had been stabbed four times in the neck and 17 times in the upper body, and she was surrounded by a large pool of blood. As she had been so brutally murdered, her intestines were exposed and hanging out. Forensics turned up fingerprints that matched Lockhart's DNA.

Lockhart was a multi-state serial killer who became infamous for receiving three different death sentences in three different states. He had killed in Florida, Indiana, and Texas. He was arrested in 1988 and sentenced to death. In 1997 he was executed in Texas while still on death row in two other States.

October 15th

In Southern England and Northern France, *The Great Storm of 1987* caused widespread disruption and deaths. It was a cyclone that occurred on the night of the 15th and continued into the 16th with hurricane-force winds. From London to the North Coast of France, extreme winds battered the region.

The British *National Power Grid* suffered immense damage leaving thousands of homes without power. Ancient trees were ripped up and thrown across roads and railways, and parks were destroyed. Approximately 15 million trees were uprooted. The winds reached 135 miles per hour (217 kilometres per hour).

Famously, the BBC weatherman, Michael Fish, stated before the storm that reports of high winds were a false alarm.

"Earlier on today, apparently, a woman rang the BBC and said she heard there was a hurricane on the way; well, if you're watching, don't worry, there isn't."

Michael Fish, BBC weatherman.

It has since become a national gaffe, however the weather reports coming in showed no signs of such a storm. It is known as a weather bomb due to the speed it developed.

22 people were killed across England and France and hundreds more were injured. As a result of the storm, improvements were made in satellite tracking, computer modelling and weather reporting.

October 19th

Black Monday, the day of the Wall Street crash. Stock markets around the world take a massive hit. It started in Hong Kong and followed the time zone across to the United States. The *Dow Jones Industrial Average* (DJIA) dropped by over 22%. Multiple causes have been given over the years including program trading and overvaluation.

October 26th

American medical serial killer *Donald Harvey*, AKA: *The Angel of Death*, was admitted to the *Toledo Correctional Institution* in Ohio on this day. This was after being convicted in August 1987 of killing 37 people. Harvey was a hospital orderly who claimed to have murdered 87 people between 1970 to April 1987, when he was arrested.

Harvey claimed to have begun killing only to ease the pain of his patients, but stated that as time progressed his enjoyment rose. He was given 28 life sentences after pleading guilty in order to avoid the death penalty. In 2017, he was badly beaten in his cell and died of his injuries on March 30th of that year.

October 29th

In Los Angeles, 26-year-old *Annette Ernest* was found dead along the hard shoulder near Grand Avenue and 106th Street in Vermont Vista. She had been raped and strangled to death by American serial killer *Chester DeWayne Turner*.

In 2007, he was first convicted of killing 10 women from 1987 to 1998, in addition to the death of an unborn child. By 2014 he was convicted of another four murders, bringing his total to 15 victims, and suspected of many more. He is known to be one of the most prolific serial killers in the city of Los Angeles.

He received death sentences in both trials and as of 2019, he currently remains on death row.

October 31st

On Halloween 1987, American serial killer *Daniel Lee Corwin* stabs to death 36-year-old *Mary Carrell Risinger* at a car wash. He had attempted to abduct her but she fought back and screamed for help. Corwin then stabbed her in the neck as her three-year-old daughter looked on from inside the car. She bled to death at the scene.

He killed three people, all in 1987, but the seeds were laid 12 years earlier. In 1975 when he was just 17-years-old, Corwin abducted a classmate from his high school. He bound her in his car, drove her to a remote area and raped her. Then he dragged her from the car, beat her and stabbed her in the heart. Miraculously, she survived and pulled herself to a road to get help.

Corwin was sentenced to 40 years in prison but astonishingly paroled after just nine years of the sentence served. He was released in November of 1985 and then went on to kill only 16 months later in February of 1987.

Corwin was convicted of three 1987 murders, sentenced to death and executed by lethal injection in December of 1988.

Norman Simons – *The Station Strangler*

South African serial killer *Norman Avzal Simons*, killed at least 22 young boys between 1986 and 1994. He was convicted on one of the murders and is part of an ongoing court process to this day. By 1994, the residents of *Mitchell's Plain* were haunted by the plague of a serial killer known as *The Station Strangler*.

South Africa in 1994 was going through a process of rebirth and struggle. Apartheid had fallen and the country was about to celebrate the news by holding its first democratic elections. For a large number of families, the new freedom meant very little because their children were dead, and the killer was still walking their streets.

During his childhood, Simons was deemed to be an intelligent boy who played classical instruments such as the piano. He also learned and spoke seven languages and went on to a career in teaching. He taught Grade-five students, which is generally children aged between 10-years-old to 11-years-old. It is no surprise then that most of his victims were around that age group.

He is known to be South Africa's *Andrei Chikatilo* and was even inspired by the stories coming out of Russia. Chikatilo was a Russian serial killer who killed young boys and girls by mostly luring them away from train stations. Simons utilised the same method and thus became known as *The Station Strangler*. He is to this day, one of South Africa's most notorious serial killers.

Simons claimed that during his formative years, his older stepbrother raped him on many occasions. His brother was an alcoholic Rastafarian who was murdered in 1991 in a separate incident. Simons also claimed that he heard his brother's voice in his head, ordering him to kill others.

His brother then moved from voices to possession. His spirit jumped into Simons body and lived inside him, ordering him to kill. He claims that the voices and delusions began when his brother started to rape him. He refrained from acting on the voices until 1986.

He claimed his first victim in that year when he was just 19-years-old. He lured 14-year-old *Jonathan Claasen* away from *Modderdam Station*, before raping and killing him. Claasen's body was discovered on October 3rd 1986. Generally, Simons would tie their hands behind their backs and strangle them with their own underwear. He would dump the bodies near to the stations in shallow graves with the corpses laying face down.

The area of Mitchell's Plain is 20 miles from Cape Town and is one of South Africa's largest suburbs. It was a large housing area that quickly became an urban ghetto. The transition from housing projects to ghetto came about because of poverty, drugs and a rising criminal underclass. Children were still free to roam and play around until the bodies began to pile up.

On January 7th 1987, the body of 10-year-old *Yussuf Hoffmann* was discovered. He had been killed in the exact same manner. Hoffman had been raped and strangled to death with a piece of his own clothing. His hands were tied behind his back and his face had been pushed into the sand in the area of Rocklands.

On January 23rd 1987, the body of 13-year-old *Mario Thomas* was discovered in Kuilsriver, less than 20 miles away from the location of Hoffman's body. It was already becoming clear that a perverse serial killer was stalking the streets of Mitchell's Plain.

In June 1987, 12-year-old *Freddie Cleaves* was discovered near *Belhar Train Station*, just six miles away from the body of Mario Thomas. In August 1987, the body of 14-year-old *Samuel Ngaba* was discovered at the exact same station as Cleave's body.

On October 1st 1987, the seventh victim was discovered almost a year to the day of the discovery of the first victim. The unnamed boy was found in exactly the same location as Simons very first victim, at Modderdam Railway Station.

By the beginning of 1988, nine young boys had been found murdered in the same fashion and the community of Mitchell's Plain was in a state of panic and fear.

Serial killers were and are rare in South Africa, despite the huge amount of crime in the country. And so the local detective assigned to the case had no experience or training in how to solve serial killing cases.

Because of the public knowledge of the killings, the murders ceased for a number of years until 1992 when The Station Strangler returned to his old stomping ground of Mitchell's Plain and began killing again. The body of an 11-year-old boy was found in October of 1992, face down on a local beach.

It wasn't until January 1994 that he would kill again in what came to be known as the *month of horror*. It began on January 13th, when the body of an unidentified young boy was discovered in the remote *Weltevrede Dunes* outside of Cape Town. The dunes were considered remote enough that bodies would be hard to find.

Like the *Texas Killing Fields* in the United States, the Weltevrede Dunes became The Station Strangler's killing fields. Every victim from then onwards would be found in the dunes. Even up until 2019, they have become synonymous with the murders.

Once the first body had been found, more bodies began turning up on the dunes. The community was in shock and demanded action, so the police began searching the dunes themselves. Over the month of January 1994, in conjunction with the *South African Army*, the police discovered a total of 11 bodies on the Weltevrede Dunes.

On January 27th alone, six bodies were uncovered on the dunes. One was an adult male killed in the same fashion and the other 10 were of young boys. In February 1994, a special task team consisting of 14 men was set up, called the *Station Strangler Squad*. The task team was given every resource available and even had help from FBI serial killer profiler *Robert Ressler*.

Ressler was set on heading to South Africa to assist the team but the political unrest in the country at the time put him off and in the end he remained in the States. Ressler reviewed some of the profiles drawn up about The Station Strangler and mostly agreed with what had been written. He would later go to a South African press conference where he would praise the investigatory team on their work.

On April 13th 1994, Norman Simons was arrested in connection with another murdered boy who had been discovered on the Weltevrede Dunes in March. He would go on to confess that he had been killing young boys since 1986. An officer with no knowledge of the case was brought in to accompany Simons as they undertook a walk-through of the dunes.

Simons pointed out where the bodies had been found and even showed him areas where other bodies should have been. He pointed out an area in the dunes where he stated he killed another boy. No body was found there but items of clothing were recovered. It was also known that wild animals would come to the dunes to hunt and it was suggested that more bodies may have been consumed by them.

"I am nothing. I am dirty. I am filthy and not worthy. I am sorry for letting you down. Don't get caught in the same thing. I really regret everything. It's hard to be possessed by unknown forces. These forces cannot be explained by medication."

Norman Simons – from his confession.

The trial began in 1995 and lasted three months. Because of lack of evidence due to decomposition of the bodies, they were only able to convict him on the final victim in March of 1994 based on eye-witness reports. He was sentenced to life and is currently incarcerated at the *Drakenstein Maximum Correctional Facility* in Paarl, the same prison were Nelson Mandela was imprisoned.

Further prosecutions were ruled out and Simons repeatedly appealed his conviction but the sentence was upheld at every juncture. An inquest in 2005, led Simons defence team to claim his innocence in the crimes. There is now a public perception that the wrong killer may have been caught and that Simons was merely a copycat killer.

It was alleged that even during his trial, more boys had gone missing and more bodies were found. Although this is in hearsay, there is a huge belief in it and also in the conspiracy that authorities covered up the subsequent murders to not look inept in the eyes of the community. However in 2008, the inquest ended and it was suggested there was sufficient evidence for Simons being the killer in at least some of the murders.

The next heading goes into the belief that Norman Simons was not the *true* Station Strangler.

Brian Shofer – *The 2nd Station Strangler?*

In 2014, a man who testified to being a surviving victim of *The Station Strangler*, claimed that *Norman Simons* was not the man who had attacked him. He and a friend were lured to a remote area and raped with an attempt to strangle them. When the man had fallen asleep, they both managed to escape.

Because their friends knew Norman Simons, they were sure that he was not the man who attacked them. The man who attacked them was apparently known to police but was never questioned in the investigation for the murders.

A short while later, a radio station in Cape Town was debating the case live on air when they received a phone call from one of the prosecutors, *Mike Stowe*, who was involved in the original trial. He claimed live on air that he was sure they had convicted the wrong man.

He claimed that witness statements didn't add up and that no one had seen Simons near the train stations when the boys had gone missing. He also cited further information that he felt was inconclusive.

Stowe's conversation and admission of possible innocence sent shock waves through the country and especially the area of Mitchell's Plains. Family members of the victims were in uproar and suddenly the entire Station Strangler story was thrown into confusion.

In 2016, 58-year-old *Brian Shofer* killed himself in his police cell. Shofer was a convicted South African paedophile who had been arrested just two days prior for the rape of a 17-year-old boy. The boy in question had been living with Shofer since he was 12-years-old. Shofer spent a lifetime surrounding himself with children and taught children in his home, or theirs, under a private tutorship.

Shofer was a resident in Mitchell's Plain at the same time that the Station Strangler was active. Shofer claimed that he was violently abused as a child and that his uncle raped him on numerous occasions. His father knew of the abuse and allowed it to happen. He also claimed that from this abuse, he grew to prefer children as sexual contacts.

Shortly after a 2010 conviction for sexual assault, he began working at a primary school in the Cape Town area. He left shortly after when his landlords claimed that Shofer had been in a relationship with a 16-year-old girl. Both of them happened to believe that he was the real strangler. Even as far back as 1994, Shofer had been found guilty of multiple rapes on young boys under the age of 15-years-old.

Before he killed himself, Shofer was about to be charged with 18 cases of sexual assault involving homeless children and runaways. After his death, some criminal profilers came forward who suggested there were two serial killers, who had exactly the same process of killing young boys.

The inquest into Norman Simons concluded that there was sufficient evidence to link him to at least six of the murders but not good enough evidence to link him to the rest. But because he had pointed out the murder scenes and one other where clothes were found, then it is generally assumed that Simons *is* The Station Strangler, regardless of the minimal evidence that convicted him.

If there was a second strangler or an accomplice then it is also generally assumed to be Shofer. However, he now takes his secrets to the grave and the end of the story remains solely with Norman Simons – The Station Strangler.

November 1987

November 1st

In Los Angeles, the body of 26-year-old *Mary Lowe* is discovered in Gramercy Park. She had been raped and shot dead by LA-based serial killer *Lonnie David Franklin Jr.* When he was arrested in 2010, he had claimed at least ten victims but is suspected and linked to a possible 25.

Franklin killed seven people from 1985 to 1988 but then came a 14 year gap when there were no killings. He then killed again three more times from 2002 to 2007. The gap between the killings earned him the notorious moniker of *The Grim Sleeper,* given to him by a reporter who wrote a story on the murders of black women in the area.

November 8th

In Northern Ireland, *The Remembrance Day Bombing* also known as *The Poppy Day Massacre* takes place. A *Provisional Irish Republican Army* (IRA) bomb exploded near the town's war memorial during a Remembrance Sunday ceremony. 11 people, mostly elderly, were killed and 63 were injured.

The IRA later claimed it had intended to kill British Soldiers on a Remembrance Sunday parade but had made a mistake and apologised to the victims. They made authorities aware of a second bomb which was disarmed before potentially having killed up to 80 children who were near it at the time.

November 13th

In England, *Robert Melias* becomes the first person in the world to be convicted of a crime using DNA evidence. He had been found guilty of rape and convicted by a British court. Scientists calculated that the chance of the sample from the crime scene not coming from Melias was 1 in 4 million of the male population.

Following Melias's conviction and in the same month, *Tommy Lee Andrews* became the first American to be convicted on DNA evidence. Andrews was also charged with rape, in Florida.

November 15th

American medical serial killer *Richard Angelo* is arrested and taken into custody after assaulting a 73-year-old patient of his. By the time of his arrest, Angelo was only 25-years-old and had killed at least eight people.

Sometimes referred to as the *Angel of Death*, Angelo was a nurse at the *Good Samaritan Hospital* in the Suffolk County area of New York. He used poison to kill and was linked with at least ten deaths, and the poisoning of at least 25 others. He poisoned his victims to bring on a cardiac arrest so that he could try and resuscitate them in front of other workers at the hospital. He claimed he did it in order to be seen as a hero.

Angelo was convicted in December 1989 for two of the murders, one manslaughter, and one criminally negligent homicide. In four other deaths he was convicted of associated assault. It is suspected that he killed at least 10. Angelo was sentenced to at least 50 years in prison and currently remains incarcerated at the *Great Meadow Correctional Facility* in Washington County.

November 18th

In Illinois, police descend on a mobile home in the village of *Ina*. Inside they find an entire family has been slaughtered. 29-year-old *Russell Keith Dardeen* was found in a nearby field, he had been shot and his genitals were mutilated. His pregnant wife and son who were in the mobile home were beaten to death. *Ruby Elaine Dardeen* was so badly beaten that she went into labour. Shockingly, the newborn was also beaten to death.

Convicted serial killer *Tommy Lynn Sells* who was on death row for separate murders confessed to the killing of the Dardeen family. He had been convicted of two murders but was suspected of at least another 10. Sells claimed he killed over 70 people but his claims have always been doubted. He was executed on April 3rd 2014.

The investigation into the Dardeen murders is currently an active cold case.

On the same day.

In London, a fire breaks out at *King's Cross St Pancras* tube station, a major interchange on the *London Underground*. The fire started under a wooden escalator on the Piccadilly Line and then erupted into the underground ticket hall. The fire left 31 people dead and injured over 100.

On the same day.

A young couple on an overnight trip to Seattle, 20-year-old *Jay Cook* and 18-year-old *Tanya Van Cuylenborg*, were savagely murdered. When they didn't return as planned, their parents filed missing person reports. A week later, Cuylenborg's partially naked body was found in a ditch in Skagit County. She had been raped and killed with a single gunshot to the back of the head.

Two days after her body had been found, Cook's body was discovered underneath a bridge, 60 miles away from where Cuylenborg was found. He had been battered to death with nearby rocks, and was found with a ligature of plastic twine and two red dog collars around his neck.

The murders remained unsolved until 2017 when investigators in Snohomish County, Washington, turned to genetic genealogy to solve the murders. It involved a combination of DNA analysis and family tree research. On May 17th 2018, they charged a 56-year-old man with both murders.

As of June 2019, the jury has just been selected for the impending trial.

November 20th

Infamous serial killer, *Jeffrey Dahmer*, AKA: *The Milwaukee Cannibal*, kills 25-year-old *Steven Tuomi* in a rented room at the *Ambassador Hotel* in Milwaukee. Dahmer had met Tuomi at a bar and persuaded him back to the hotel room.

He drugged Tuomi with an intention to render him useless but not kill him. Dahmer awoke to find him dead as he lay on top of him. He claims he had no memory of the murder and that he must have been drugged in order to have beaten the man to death.

He bought a large suitcase and took the body to his grandmother's house where he was living at the time. A week later he beheaded Tuomi and dismembered him. He cut small chunks of flesh away from the bones so he could dispose of them in the trash. He then wrapped the bones in bags and smashed them with a sledgehammer to turn them into dust. He claims it took him two hours to complete the process.

Dahmer kept Tuomi's head in a blanket, but after two weeks he decided to boil the head and us a process of bone-cleaning his father had taught him, so that he could retain the skull. Other times, the process worked but in this instance, it caused the skull to become brittle, so he disposed of it shortly after.

Dahmer killed 17 people between 1978 and 1991 and was convicted with 16 life sentences. He was murdered in prison in 1994 by a fellow inmate. A more detailed run down of Dahmer's life can be found in the preceding book in this series.

Timothy Wilson Spencer – *The Southside Strangler*

On **November 22**nd, 15-year-old high school student *Diane Cho*, was found dead in her family's, in Chesterfield County. She had been raped and strangled by serial killer *Timothy Wilson Spencer*, AKA: *The Southside Strangler.* Spencer would be convicted of five murders from 1984 to 1987, and was the first serial killer in the United States to be convicted on DNA evidence.

His case also involved the first person to be found innocent of a crime they had previously been convicted for, all because of the advances in DNA technology.

Born in 1962, Spencer was raised in the Green Valley area of Arlington, Virginia. At the time, it was generally a black neighbourhood and known as a lower-income region area prone to violence.

In 1984, Spencer claimed his first victim, *Carolyn Hamm*, from Virginia. Her body was discovered face down near the door to her garage. She had been raped, tied up and hung with a cord from a Venetian blind. Her murder was in an area where violent crime was considered rare, and due to media attention, an arrest was made quickly. A confession was obtained and charges were brought to *David Vasquez.*

Vazquez was wrongly convicted and served five years of a 35 year prison sentence before the conviction was overturned in 1989. He was the first person to have his conviction overturned due to advancements in DNA technology.

On November 27th 1987, Spencer murdered 44-year-old *Susan Tucker* who was strangled to death in her condominium. The body wasn't discovered until December 1st. In a similar fashion to the 1984 murder, a cord had been taken from a nearby Venetian blind and used to strangled her. She had also been raped and her body had been found nude, partially covered by a sleeping bag.

In both cases, the killer had entered the properties through a first floor window and it was suggested that due to the prevalence of semen stains that Spencer had masturbated over the bodies. An investigation then linked three more murders that were carried out in 1987, over a hundred miles away in Richmond

On September 19th 1987, in Richmond, *Debbie Davis* was found dead in her first floor apartment which she lived in alone. She had been strangled with a sock that had been tied around her neck and twisted tight with a small section of pipe. Spencer had left multiple semen stains on Davis as well.

Just two weeks later and less than a mile away from the Davis crime scene, *Dr. Susan Hellams* was found dead in her bedroom closet. She had been killed in a very similar fashion to Davis and the other victims.

And then 15-year-old high school student *Diane Cho* was raped and strangled by Spencer. She had been killed in her bedroom while her family slept nearby in the other rooms. Duct tape had been put across her mouth to stop her from crying out. She too had been strangled with a ligature and semen stains were found on the body and the sheets.

It took a large effort by lead investigators to convince different departments that the murders were linked. This is referred to as *linkage blindness* and makes serial killing cases difficult to investigate. The lead investigator, *Joe Horgas*, then connected various rape and burglary cases in the region.

In one incident of burglary, Spencer had climbed through a basement window of a woman's apartment and left porn magazines in the house along with a cord from a Venetian blind on her bed. It was suggested that Spencer was waiting for her to come home but for some reason decided to leave.

After following up the burglary and rape cases, Horgas determined that Spencer's methods had been perfected over many years. Beginning with burglaries then rape and then finally moving onto murder. The pattern was becoming obvious as the crime scenes were starting to look very similar.

Spencer was arrested in 1988 and subsequently convicted of murder and rape. He was sentenced to death and executed in the electric chair on April 27th 1994. He was known to have killed five people and raped many more.

November 25th

French serial killer *Thierry Paulin* brutally murders 79-year-old *Rachel Cohen*, she would become one of his 18 accused murders. Later on the same day he brutally attacked 87-year-old woman, *Berthe Finalteri,* but she would go on to survive and give a description that would result in the capture of Paulin. The killing of *Genevieve Germont* on November 27th, would be his final victim.

Thierry Paulin had contracted HIV in the years prior and then AIDS. His killings sped up as he realised he was under a biological death sentence, and set out to cause as much carnage and chaos as possible. He organised large and expensive parties that were all paid for with stolen credit cards along with the financial gains from his murders.

He was arrested on December 1st 1987 and accused of 18 murders. He confessed to 21 killings. Just over a month later, Paulin fell ill as AIDS set in. He was subsequently hospitalised and died on April 16th 1989.

On the same day.

In Germany, 21-year-old student *Andrea Grube-Nagel* goes missing. She was the first victim to be abducted and murdered by German serial killer *Thomas Holst*, AKA: *Heidemörder.*

As Andrea was leaving the *Rissen Train Station* in Hamburg, Holst had forced her into his car by putting a knife to her throat and threatening to stab her. He raped, tortured and dismembered her as he would his next two victims. Two days later, Andrea's remains were found by construction workers in the town of Kaltenkirchen, which is just north of Hamburg.

Over a two year period from November 1987 to November 1989, Thomas Holst abducted, raped and killed three women from Hamburg. Upon his arrest a psychiatric stated that he was '*untreatable and with extreme relapse probability*.' He was sent to trial for the violent murders of three victims and subsequently to a high-security wing of a psychiatric hospital.

Astonishingly, his therapist, *Tamar Segal*, helped him escape in 1995 as she had fallen in love with him. Holst gave himself up three months later and was detained at the *Hamburg Detention Center* where he has been ever since. In another bizarre twist, Thomas Holst married Segal while he was in prison in 1997 and by all accounts they are still married to this day.

On the same day.

In Pima County, Arizona, the body of 16-year-old *Deanna Lee Criswell* was found, she had been shot in the head. She remained a Jane Doe until 2015 when advancements in facial recognition, DNA, and missing persons websites identified her. Before her identification, a cold case had linked a spree robber to the murder but he died in 2005, leaving the investigation at a dead end.

On the same day.

In the United States, '*Three Men and a Baby*' is released. It goes on to become the biggest film in the country in 1987, taking in $167million USD at the domestic box office. It is the fifth biggest film in the world in 1987 and was achieved only through domestic (USA) ticket sales, as the film was not released to the international market until half a year later.

On the same day.

In the Philippines, *Typhoon Nina* struck the island of Luzon. It was the strongest tropical cyclone to strike the region in many years and left 812 people dead in its wake. By November 20th, a growing storm became a tropical storm when it hit the Chuuk Lagoon. The storm killed four people there and left thousands homeless on the atoll's islands.

It became a full typhoon the next day and then tracked towards

Luzon. It quickly approached the island with 165 mph (265 kph) sustained winds. It battered the islands for the next 18 hours as it passed over, barely easing up until it dissipated over the sea.

November 27th

French serial killer *Thierry Paulin* claims his final victim. He strangled to death *Genevieve Germont*. Paulin was accused of 18 murders but confessed to 21. He died of AIDS related illnesses in 1989 while awaiting trial.

On the same day.

In Kaltenkirchen, Germany, 21-year-old student *Andrea Grube-Nagel's* remains are found by construction workers. She is the first victim of serial killer *Thomas Holst.* She had been abducted, raped, tortured and dismembered. Holst was convicted of three murders and remains in the *Hamburg Detention Center* to this day.

On the same day.

In Virginia, 44-year-old, *Susan Tucker*, is killed in her condominium. Her body wasn't found until December 1st 1987. She had been raped and strangled by serial killer *Timothy Wilson Spencer*, AKA: *The Southside Strangler.* Spencer was the first serial killer in the United States to be convicted on DNA evidence.

November 29th

Mississippi murderer *Earl Wesley Berry* brutally beats to death church choir member *Mary Bounds*. She was kidnapped after leaving choir practice, driven to a wooded area and beaten to death. Berry claimed he intended to commit rape but decided to kill her instead.

He was arrested in December 1987 and sentenced to death for the murder. He was put to death on May 21st 2008, by lethal injection. He showed no remorse for his crimes and had he not been caught after murder one, it is suggested he would have continued killing. His last words were: "*No comment.*"

On the same day.

Prostitute *Shirley Ellis* was picked up by American serial killer *Steven Brian Pennell*, with the promise of money for sex in his van. He then tied Ellis up, brutally raped, beat and mutilated her. Her body was dumped near Route 40.

Also known as *The Route 40 Killer*, Pennell killed five people in the State of Delaware, where he is infamous for being the State's only known serial killer. His victims mostly consisted of hitchhikers and prostitutes who he picked up in his work van.

He was arrested in 1988 and convicted of two murders. He pleaded no contest on three more murders on the condition that he be executed as a preference. There was another murder in 1988 that he was also linked to but not proven. He claimed that it would be easier to execute him rather than have his family see him in jail for the rest of his life. In 1992,

Pennell was executed by lethal injection, the first to be executed in Delaware since 1946, almost 50 years later.

DNA Evidence Exploded in the 1980s

In England, on **November 13th** 1987, *Robert Melias* becomes the first person to be convicted of a crime using DNA evidence. He had been found guilty of rape and convicted by a British court. Scientists calculated that the chance of the sample from the crime scene *not* coming from Melias was 1 in 4 million of the male population.

Following Melias's conviction and in the same month, *Tommy Lee Andrews* became the first American to be convicted on DNA evidence. Andrews was also charged with rape, in Florida.

DNA profiling was originally developed as a method of determining paternity that could link a child with a parent. But it was the Robert Melias case in England that changed it all. The investigation had sought the help of a molecular biologist named *Alec Jeffreys,* as he had begun to use DNA for forensic testing. The perpetrator was caught based on the DNA evidence and subsequently convicted because of it.

In Florida, Tommy Lee Andrews was convicted because DNA tests found a match from his blood and semen in a rape victim. In the years that followed, no one disputed or argued against DNA evidence in criminal trials. As soon as prosecutors began using DNA to convict then defence lawyers began questioning the admissibility of DNA.

During the late 1980s and early 1990s, there were a number of legal challenges against DNA evidence. The challenges against DNA evidence mostly arose because the validity of the techniques used were coming under scrutiny. Out of these cases came a national standard for collecting DNA evidence.

In many cases, a DNA testing laboratory protocol's would be brought into question. Their validation processes were deemed insufficient, meaning evidence was denied. Once lawful protocol's came into place then DNA testing would become common in criminal cases that required DNA as evidence.

The federal *DNA Identification Act of 1994*, meant that DNA profiles could be held on record for a set amount of time. It meant that laboratories had to adhere to a strict set of protocols for testing and uploading profiles to the database. In the same year, these protocols became uniform standards when the *Violent Crime Control and Law Enforcement Act* was implemented.

In the late 1990s and through the 2000s, the DNA databases helped solved a number of cold cases from the 1970s onwards. In 2002, Virginia became the first state to execute a criminal based on DNA evidence assisting in a cold case investigation. *James Earl Patterson* was already serving time for rape when he was linked to the murder.

The ability to use DNA testing to convict and to exonerate suspects changed the way that criminals were convicted, especially in rape and murder cases. It is now one of the most powerful tools that it used within the criminal justice system.

December 1987

December 1st

French serial killer *Thierry Paulin* was arrested while walking down the street. His surviving victim, 87-year-old *Berthe Finalteri*, who he'd attacked on November 25th had given investigators a detailed description.

He was spotted and caught by an officer not long after his final murder on November 27th. Paulin was accused of 18 murders but confessed to 21. He died of AIDS related illnesses in 1989 while awaiting trial.

On the same day.

In California, 30-year-old *Deborah Jackson* was murdered by serial killer *Michael Hughes*, AKA: the *Southside Slayer*. He killed seven females between the ages of 15-years-old to 38-years-old over a six year period from 1986 to his arrest in 1993.

In two separate trials he was convicted of the murders of all seven and given the death sentence in June 2012. As of 2019, he remains on death row at *San Quentin State Prison* in California.

December 3ʳᵈ

Russian serial killer *Nikolai Arkadievich Dudin*, AKA: *The Grim Maniac*, shoots dead his father. He hid the body for an entire year, but an arrest for rape saw him confess to the murder. He was only 13-years-old when he killed his father. Due to his age he escaped the death sentence and was imprisoned, where he incited riots along with an attempted murder.

He was released in 2000, and two years later killed another 12 people in various incidents. He would use guns, knifes and blunt objects to kill his victims. After being caught red-handed in the act of murder, he was arrested and sentenced to life imprisonment. He was sent to a special regime colony, the *Supermax White Swan Prison*, where he remains to this day.

December 7ᵗʰ

Over California, a disgruntled airline employee, 35-year-old *David Augustus Burke* crashed a commercial airline, killing 43 people on board. The flight; *Pacific Southwest Airlines Flight 1771* was on a routine daily journey from Los Angeles to San Francisco.

Burke had recently been fired from *USAir* over petty theft, by his supervisor, *Ray Thomson.* Burke purchased a ticket for the flight knowing that Thomson would be on board. Using his still active USAir documents he was able to bypass security with a loaded *.44 Magnum* pistol. When the plane was at 22,000 feet, Burke shot Thomson before moving to the cockpit and shooting the pilots.

The black box recording picked up a final gun shot just before it went silent and it was suspected that Burke had shot himself dead before the plane went down. The plane crashed at a cattle ranch and there were no survivors.

December 8th

In Australia, *The Queen Street Massacre* takes place. Half-Croatian, half-Italian *Frank Vitkovic* entered the *Australia Post Offices* in Melbourne carrying a sawn-off semi-automatic carbine gun in a brown paper bag. He strolled up to the fifth floor and began firing into the office.

A robbery alarm was activated and Vitkovic calmly took an elevator to the twelfth floor to kill more people in the offices there. He then ran back down the stairs firing randomly at anyone he saw. Then he charged into the computer training centre to kill another victim before finding several office workers in the corner of the room, who he shot at close range.

"Today is going to be the day. The anger in my head has got too much for me. I've got to get rid of my violent impulses. The time has come to die. There is no other way out."

From Vitkovic's suicide note.

Two heroes saved the day, and both had been shot. *Frank Carmody* had been shot once and *Tony Gioia* had been shot multiple times. Together they managed to overcome Vitkovic and take the gun from him. Vitkovic then tried to escape through a window and climb to the floor above. Gioia held onto his ankles to keep him back but Vitkovic fell to his death.

Both Carmody and Gioia were awarded the *Star of Courage*, an Australian bravery medal. It is claimed that Vitkovic was in some part influenced by the August 9th 1987 *Hoddle Street Massacre*, also in Melbourne, as he had newspaper cuttings of it in his home. Vitkovic killed nine people and injured five more.

December 10th

A squirrel burrows through a telephone line and shuts down the entire *Nasdaq Stock Exchange*. A nutty bushy-tailed rodent chewed through a cable and cut power to the town of Trumbull, where the Nasdaq's main trading systems were located at the time.

And it wouldn't be the last time! In 1994, those pesky nut-hoarding tree-climbers did it again and shut the Nasdaq for over half an hour. Clearly, the squirrel population of Trumbull took offence to the stock markets being in their town.

December 11th

17-year-old, *Isabelle Laville* becomes a victim of the *Ogre of the Ardennes*. French serial killer *Michel Paul Fourniret* confessed to killing 11 people in France and Belgium between 1987 and 2001. His wife *Monique Pierrette Olivier* was complicit in some of the murders and would be sentenced alongside him.

On this day in 1987 he was driving with his wife in two separate cars in a deliberate attempt to hunt their 17-year-old victim. They had spotted

Isabelle a day earlier as she was walking home from school. They had set up a plan where Isabelle got into his wife's car to give directions. Then they stopped at Fourniret's car, that would appear to be broken down at the side of the road.

His wife then stopped her car and got out to see if he needed any help. When Isabelle approached, Fourniret raped and beat her before strangling her to death. They both then threw her body down a disused well. Fourniret was arrested in 2003 and confessed to killing eight females and one male. He was convicted of seven murders and sentenced to life. His wife was sentenced to 28 years

It wouldn't be until July 11th 2006, when Isabelle Laville's remains would be recovered.

On the same day.

In the United Kingdom, *Harold Shipman* murders 80-year-old *Margaret Townsend* from Hyde, England. She was his sixth of eight victims in 1987 alone and one of three in December 1987.

On the same day.

In Spain, the Basque separatist organisation *ETA*, explode a car bomb in Zaragoza. The vehicle which held 250 kilograms of explosives was parked beside the main Guardia Civil barracks in the city.

The explosion left 11 people dead, including five children, and 88 injured. The attack came just six months after ETA had killed 21 people with a car bomb at a shopping centre in Barcelona.

December 20th

In the Philippines, the deadliest peacetime maritime disaster in history happens. The *MV Doña Paz* was a Philippine-registered passenger ferry that sank after colliding with the oil tanker *MT Vector*.

On route to Manila from Leyte island, the vessel had over 2,500 extra passengers who were not listed on any manifest. The capacity was 1,518 but there were over 4,000 people on board. It had been suggested that the life-jackets were locked away to make space for more people.

Officially, the blame was laid at Vector's feet, as the ship was found to have been unseaworthy, operating without a license and without a qualified captain. When the two ships collided, the oil tanker exploded sending fireballs through the passenger ship. A survivor later stated that the sea was on fire because of the oil.

Both ships sank in 545 meters (1,788 ft) of water in the shark-infested *Tablas Strait*. There was an estimated death toll of 4,386 people with only 24 survivors. It became known as Asia's Titanic.

December 22nd

American mass-murderer, *Ronald Gene Simmons*, murdered seven members of his family in one pre-meditated attack. And it didn't stop there, on Boxing Day, just four days later, he murdered another seven family members. On the 28th December, he walked into town and shot two more random people dead.

On the morning of the 22nd, he killed his son first and then his wife. Then he strangled his three-year-old granddaughter, dumped all their bodies in a cesspit and waited for the other children to return home. He told the arriving four children that he had a present for them but wanted to show them individually. He led them one by one to a rain barrel where he drowned them in quick succession. See December 26th for the rest of the family murders.

Simmons was arrested on December 28th, charged with 16 counts of murder, and sentenced to death. On June 25th 1990, he was executed by lethal injection.

December 26th

American mass-murderer, *Ronald Gene Simmons*, murdered another seven members of his family in a pre-meditated attack. This was in addition to the seven murdered on December 22nd.

At noon, his remaining family members arrived for their Christmas visit. He shot dead his other son and his sons wife. Then he shot their son, their daughter and her husband. He strangled a child birthed by his own daughter and then strangled his grandson.

After he had killed 14 members of his family, he went to a local bar to celebrate Christmas. Then returned home and sat all the corpses with him in the lounge area. He proceeded to continue drinking and watching television with the bodies around him.

December 28th

After killing 14 members of his family on December 22nd and 26th, he drove into town in Russellville and shot dead a law office receptionist and oil company office worker. He shot and wounded two people in a convenience store and went to the office of a motor freight company.

He shot and wounded a woman before sitting down and chatting calmly with another secretary. He waited for the police to arrive and then surrendered with no resistance. He was charged with sixteen counts of murder, and sentenced to death. On 25th June, 1990, he was executed by lethal injection.

December 29th

Just in time for the New Year, the antidepressant *Prozac* is prescribed for the first time. Prozac is used for the treatment of major depressive disorder, obsessive compulsive disorder, bulimia, and anxiety amongst others. In 2016, in the United States alone, it was prescribed over 23 million times.

On the same day.

In the United Kingdom, *Harold Shipman* kills 69-year-old Nellie Bardsley from Hyde, England. She was his seventh of eight victims in 1987. Shipman was convicted of 215 murders and is the most prolific serial killer in history.

December 30th

Just one day after his last victim, *Harold Shipman* kills again. This time he ends the life of 74-year-old *Elizabeth Ann Rogers* from Hyde. She becomes his last victim in 1987, but he would kill at least 215 people before his arrest in 1998. He killed himself in prison in 2004 and remains the most prolific serial killer in history by confirmed victims.

December 31st

A triple murder on New Years Eve rocks Wichita and remains unsolved to this day. The mother of the Fager family, *Mary Fager*, returned home in time for New Years after being away for three days. She found her entire family had been brutally murdered.

Phillip Fager, her husband, was laying face down on the living room floor having been shot dead. He was wearing a coat and so it has long been assumed he walked back into the house and caught a killer in the act. A killer who had targeted his two daughters.

16-year-old *Kelli Fager* had been drowned in the family's hot tub. Nine-year-old *Sherri Fager* had been strangled and tied up nearby. A few days later, the first suspect was arrested, a contractor named *William Butterworth* who was working on renovations on the Fager's house.

The investigation found that he had emptied his bank accounts, stole the Fager's car and drove to Florida. During his trial he was put under hypnosis and claimed that he had found the girl's already dead when he turned up at the house. He was so shocked but what he had seen that he had lost all memory of the day and eloped to Florida. It is unclear whether the father was already dead at the time he left or was killed after. Lack of evidence saw him acquitted of the murders.

Then people began to suspect the *BTK Killer*, who was later found to be *Dennis Rader*. Because Rader wanted to remain in the public eye, he sent a letter to Mary Fager claiming that he had not killed her family but admired the murderer for the way he had killed.

As of 2019, the Fager murders remain unsolved and remain open as a cold case investigation.

Michel Paul Fourniret – *The Ogre of the Ardennes*

On **December 11**th 1987, 17-year-old, *Isabelle Laville* was the first victim to be murdered by the *Ogre of the Ardennes*. French serial killer *Michel Paul Fourniret* confessed to killing 11 people in France and Belgium between 1987 and 2001. His wife *Monique Pierrette Olivier* was complicit in some of the murders and would be sentenced alongside him.

It wouldn't be until July 11th 2006, when Isabelle Laville's remains would be recovered.

Born in 1942, in the middle of World War Two, he grew up in a poor household and the threat of violence hanging over the family's head. Michel stated that in his formative years he had sexual encounters with his mother. The continuing abuse caused him a great deal of trauma and he began to develop an unhealthy view of women as he went through puberty.

He became obsessed with the notion of virginity after he discovered his first wife was not a virgin. This had upset him after learning his wife had been with other men. It was this along with his mother's incestuous abuse that led to him trying to kill mostly virgins.

His accomplice and future wife, Monique, was already aware of Michel's personality and crimes before they married. While serving time in prison for 15 counts of sexual assault against minors in and around Paris, Michel sought pen pals and placed ads in a religious magazine. Monique answered the ads and many letters were sent between them until his release from jail in 1987.

Through their letters, they developed a pact that would lead to the murders of multiple people upon his release. Michel wrote to her about his fantasy and great desire to kill virgins and young women. Monique then pledged to help Michel abduct young women and girls if he would agree to kill her abusive husband who she had separated from.

Michel never ended up killing her husband but he kept promising he would. However, Monique kept up her side of the pact and helped Michel kidnap, rape and murder multiple victims over many years.

In March 1988, Michel was contacted by 30-year-old *Farida Hammiche*, who was the wife of a convicted bank robber that Michel had shared a cell with until his release. She claimed there was cash and gold coins buried in a cemetery and she needed help to unearth it. Michel agreed and received a share of half a million French Francs (approx $87,000 USD at the time).

A month later Michel and Monique decided to steal the rest of the loot from Hammiche's apartment. They lured her out of her home and drove her to a secluded area where Michel strangled her to death. They then returned to her house to steal the rest of the haul. Hammiche's body was never found. It is unclear how much they managed to get but they purchased an expensive Château in Donchery.

In August 1988, the couple drove to a supermarket and lured 20-year-old *Fabienne Leroy* to their car. Monique was pregnant with Michel's child and pretended to be ill because of it in order to trap their next victim. They drove her to a forest near a military camp where Michel raped her and shot her in the chest. Her body was found a day later.

In January 1989, Michel took an evening train when he met 21-year-old *Jeanne-Marie Desramault*, only to learn she was staying at a convent. Once he knew her routine, he met her again at the train station two months later, this time with Monique by his side. They invited Desramault to their home and she accepted as Michel would drive her home after.

After finding out she wasn't a virgin, Michel beat her and attempted to rape her. She was gagged and strangled to death. They then buried the body in the garden of the Château. Her remains were found in 2004.

In July 1989, Michel and Monique finally married and drove to Belgian with the one-year-old son. They caught sight of 12-year-old *Elisabeth Brichet* and they waited for her to leave her friend's house. Michel asked for directions to a doctor's surgery, and she agreed to go with them in the car. The following day, Michel strangled her in their home and buried her in the garden of the Château close to where Desramault had been buried.

Her disappearance became prime time news and a number of sightings of her were recorded in the years that followed. Many suspects were put forward including *Marc Dutroux* who was an infamous child killer at the time. After Dutroux's arrest in 1996, the mother of Elisabeth Brichet organised a march in honour of the missing and murdered children of Belgium. Elisabeth's body was found the same day as Desramault on July 3rd 2004.

On November 21st 1990, the couple were convicted of burglary in a court in Nantes. They left the court shortly after and drove to a shopping centre where they lured 13-year-old *Natacha Danais*, into their vehicle. They drove her to a secluded area near the coast where Michel stabbed her twice in the chest with a screwdriver. He strangled her to death and dumped her body on a beach.

Eight days later, an innocent man named *Jean Groix*, who was a neighbour of the victim, was arrested after a witness said it was his van at the shopping centre. In a bizarre twist, he was putting up members of the ETA in his home. It was suspected that the 13-year-old neighbour had found out about it and Groix silenced her by killing her. A few months later, Groix killed himself in his cell, as he couldn't face being convicted of a child's murder.

Michel later confessed that he killed two more people in France in 2000 and 2001. This came after a 10 year break from killing when they had moved to Belgium to buy a small castle. In May of 2000, he abducted 18-year-old student *Céline Saison*. He drove her back to Belgium where he raped her before strangling her and dumping the body in a wooded area. Her remains were discovered two months later.

In May of 2001, he lured 13-year-old Thai girl *Mananya Thumpong*. He drove her to a secluded wooded area, raped her and strangled her to death. Some of her bones were found almost a year later, due to wild animals having eaten the flesh of the body. While in prison, in 2018, he confessed to killing two more women in 1988 and 1990.

In 2003, an unnamed 13-year-old girl escaped Michel's clutches and she ran from his van in Belgium. She had been tied by her ankles and wrists and managed to get help. She was able to identify Michel and he was arrested in June of 2003. A year later, Monique confessed that had her husband had killed numerous people since 1987. They were both extradited to France for their trials.

They assisted the investigation and led police to the bodies of three of the four missing victims over a two year period. The trial took place in

2008 where Michel was found guilty and sentenced to life for the murders of seven of the victims whose bodies had been discovered. Monique was sentenced to life for being an accomplice in the murders. They were ordered to pay 1.5million Euros in compensation to the families of the victims.

Although convicted of seven murders, he was linked to four more bringing the total to 11 victims. It remains one of France and Belgium's most notorious cases. As of 2019, both Michel and Monique are serving their sentences in separate prisons.

<u>100</u> Serial Killers Active during 1987

The following list is in no particular order. It includes known serial killers who were active in 1987. In this case, active means a number of things.

They would have *killed* in 1987, meaning they have a confirmed or suspected murder victim in the twelve months from January to December.

They had killed before *and* after 1987, meaning that someone could kill in 1986 *and* 1988 but are still considered *active* in 1987.

It also includes serial killers who were arrested *in* 1987 but had killed victims in the years prior to their arrest. This means that up until their capture in 1987 they were still considered *active*.

1) Andrei Chikatilo

The Red Ripper of the Soviet Union killed his first victim in December of 1978. He would go on to dismember and mutilate 52 people and confessed to 56. He would sometimes remove the uterus of his victims and chew on it as he walked away.

He gouged out the eyes or broke the eye sockets in the belief his image would be retained on the eyes of his victims. He was caught in 1990 and subsequently executed. At the end of this book, there is an extended section on The Red Ripper.

Active from 1978-1990. *Soviet Union.*

Victims: 52-56

2) Jeffrey Dahmer

He would kill 17 male victims over a period of a decade. He raped, dismembered, mutilated, cannibalised and had sex with his victim's corpses.

From 1987, he would pick up men from gay bars and take them back to a hotel room and later his home. He discovered he was gay while in puberty and sought gay bars and gay bathhouses from an early age. He would drug his victims, rape them and mostly strangle them to death. It was his fascination with the corpses that would see him become infamous amongst serial killers.

Dahmer engaged multiple times in necrophilia, having sex with the corpses until *rigor mortis* had set in. He would take photographs of his victims to log each part of the dismemberment process. He would preserve the skulls and genitals for display in his home and sometimes cannibalise parts of their flesh.

By 1991, he had begun to kill on average one person each week.

When he was caught in 1991, an investigation of his home led to some horrific discoveries. Seven skulls were found in the home along with a human heart in the freezer, photographs of the stages of dismemberment, and an altar made from candles and skulls.

Active from 1978-1991. *USA.*

Victims: *17*

3) Mikhail Novosyolov

Killed 22 people between the ages of six to 50-years-old. After he had killed his first victim, he returned a few hours later to the scene of the crime and engaged in necrophilia with the corpse. Most of his victims were sexually assaulted, choked and murdered.

He would kill children and adults.

Active from 1977-1995. *Soviet Union, Tajikistan.*

Victims: *22*

4) John Rodney McRae

On September 15th 1987, in Michigan, 15-year-old *Randy Laufer* vanished. He was murdered by serial killer and paedophile *John Rodney McRae*, who killed up to five young boys between 1950 and 1997.

Back in 1950, when McRae was only 16-years-old, he killed his eight-year-old neighbour and was subsequently sentenced to life in prison to be paroled in 1972. Up until his second arrest in 1998, many children had gone missing that would soon be linked to him.

Laufer's bones were discovered on McRae's former Michigan property in 1997 and McRae was arrested shortly after. In 1998, he was sentenced to life for the Laufer murder but is suspected to have been involved in the disappearance of at least five boys in total.

In 2005, McRae died in prison of natural causes.

Active from 1950-1997. *USA.*

Victims: 5+

5) Robert Lee Yates

He would murder at least 13 prostitutes in Washington and would claim another two in Walla Walla, and one in Skagit County. Yates would have sex and do drugs with them in his van before killing them and dumping their bodies in rural locations.

All of the women died by a gunshot wound to the head. He wasn't arrested until 2000.

Active from 1975-1998. *USA.*

Victims: 16+

6) Joseph Naso

Convicted of the death of six women but claimed up to ten victims. On August 13th, 1978, a decomposing nude body had been found. Later identified as *Carmen Colon*, one of Naso's victims. In an uncanny twist, a victim attributed to '*The Alphabet Killer*' a few years earlier, was also named Carmen Colon.

He wasn't arrested until 2011, but was sentenced to death in 2013.

Active from 1977-1994. *USA.*

Victims: 6-10

7) Lorenzo Jerome Gilyard

He raped and killed 13 women and girls but was convicted of six counts of murder in 2007. He had sex with the victims, usually by force, and left their bodies in secluded or isolated locations.

All of them were strangled and struggled against him. Bizarrely, every victim was missing their shoes. Gilyard was arrested in 2004 and it is suggested many more victims could have been attributed to him.

Active from 1977-1993. *USA.*

Victims: 13

8) Edward Edwards

Born Charles Murray, Edward Wayne Edwards was suspected of murdering at least five people. He was on the FBI's Ten Most Wanted Fugitives list in 1961 for armed robberies at gas stations. He has been connected to many more crimes including the Atlanta Murders in 1979 to 1981.

Edwards was caught in 2009 but died of natural causes in 2011. He was linked many times as a suspect in the Zodiac Killer investigation.

Active from 1977-1996. *USA.*

Victims: *5+*

9) Harold Shipman

Doctor Death was one of the most prolific serial killers in history. He was found guilty of 215 murders of patients under his care. It was estimated that his total victim count would be over 250. Over 80% of his victims were elderly women and he would generally ensure that he made it on to their wills before ending their lives.

Britain's health care system was modified as a result of Shipman's crimes. Arrested in 1998, he hung himself in his cell at Wakefield Prison in January 2004. It was confirmed he killed eight patients in 1987 alone.

Active from 1975-1998. *UK.*

Victims: *215-250+*

10) Volker Eckert

A German serial killer who was convicted of killing six women in various European countries. He is known to have killed nine and accused of more murders in different countries throughout his life. Investigations were closed after he killed himself during proceedings in 2007.

In most of the murders, he would strangle the women, mutilate them and photograph them. Afterwards, he would cut off the hair and dress the corpses. He would keep the hair as trophies of his crimes.

Active from 1974-2006. *Germany, France, Spain, Italy, Czech Republic.*

Victims: *6-19+*

11) Gilbert Paul Jordan

Known as *The Boozing Barber*, he was linked to the murders of up to 10 women over a 22 year period. He used alcohol as a murder weapon. His other convictions are for rape, assault, kidnapping, hit and run and car theft.

He would seek women in bars and ply them with drink, sometimes paying them for sex. Because some of his victims were alcoholics, the police paid little attention. He was known to have drunk almost two bottles of vodka every day.

Active from 1965-2004. *Canada.*

Victims: *8-10*

12) Bible Belt Strangler

Also known as *The Redhead Murders*, the killings are a series of unidentified murders linked to an unidentified serial killer. The first victim was in October 1978 and the killings may have continued until 1992. Hardly any of the victims have been identified but most of them usually had red hair.

Their bodies were discovered along major highways across the States and they were thought to be hitchhikers or prostitutes. There is believed to be a total of six to 11 victims that have been attributed to one serial killer.

Active from 1978-1992. *USA.*

Victims: 6-11+

13) Werner Ferrari

One of Switzerland's most infamous criminals. He killed five children in the 1970s. He would lure them away or kidnap them from popular music festivals before abusing and strangling them.

He first killed a 10-year-old boy in 1971 before being arrested and serving just eight years. Between 1980 and 1989, another 11 children were abducted and eight were violently murdered. Three were never found and Ferrari denied any involvement in their disappearances.

As of 2019, he is still one of Switzerland's most notorious inmates.

Active from 1971-1989. *Switzerland.*

Victims: 5-13+

14) Fred and Rosemary West

Fred and Rosemary West would take the lives of at least 12 young women before being arrested in 1994. Their address of *25 Cromwell Street* became synonymous with the murders and became known as the House of Horrors.

So much hate was subsequently directed towards the House of Horrors, that *Gloucester City Council* intervened. They purchased the property for £40,000 GBP in 1996, in the knowledge that no one would live there. They then unceremoniously destroyed the property along with any physical trace of the horrors that had haunted the building.

The West's turned their children and some hitchhikers into sex slaves before barbarically murdering them. They mostly buried the bodies in the garden and underneath the patio of 25 Cromwell Street. They were arrested in 1994.

Active from 1967-1987. *UK.*

Victims: 12+

15) Tamara Ivanyutina

Ukrainian female serial killer murdered nine people over an 11 year period. As most female serial killers tend to do, she used poisoning as her modus operandi. From 1976, she used thallium to poison those she simply didn't like, there was no other reason. She would source thallium by saying it was to kill rats in and around hers and her parent's property.

In 1987, at a school where she was working, several pupils and staff were hospitalised for extreme food poisoning. Two adults died and nine others went to intensive care. An investigation ensued leading to her arrest and subsequent confessions going back to 1976.

She claimed she targeted the school canteen because the sixth-graders refused to set up tables and chairs and so she decided to punish them.

Executed by firing squad in 1987.

Active from 1976-1987. *Ukraine.*

16) Roger Kibbe

Also known as the *I-5 Strangler*, Kibbe would kill eight people over a decade. He would pick up hitchhikers on the highways surrounding Sacramento in California. In 1991 he was sentenced to 25 years for one murder but would go on to be convicted of the others during his time in prison.

He kidnapped his victims, tied them up and gagged them with duct tape. He would then cut open their clothes using scissors that belonged to his mother. Then Kibbe would rape them before strangling them to death. He also cut the hair of most of his victims.

As of 2019 he remains an inmate at the Mule Creek State Prison in California.

Active from 1977-1987. *USA.*

Victims: *8+*

17) Connecticut River Valley Killer

Another unidentified serial killer supposed to have begun in 1978 and ended in 1987. He or she is responsible for a series of murders in New Hampshire. The victims were mostly women and were stabbed to death.

On January 10th 1987, In Stratton, Vermont, a 38-year-old nurse named *Barbara Agnew* was stabbed to death in her car during a snowstorm. She had been returning from a skiing trip but never made it home. A snowplow driver found the car at a rest stop and went to see if the driver needed assistance.

The window was cracked and blood covered the steering wheel, but there was no one inside. Agnew wouldn't be discovered until March 28th 1987. Her body was found beside an apple tree in Windsor County, she had died at the hands of the Connecticut River Valley Killer.

Seven victims have been identified as being murders carried out by the unknown killer. There are claims that the Connecticut River Valley Killer murdered many more.

As of 2019 there have been three suspects, but the killer remains at large.

Active from 1978-1987. *USA.*

Victims: 7+

18) Howard Arthur Allen

American serial killer who killed elderly women between 1974 to 1987. The murder of 73-year-old *Ernestine Griffin* on July 14th, was particularly brutal and resulted in his capture.

The day before her murder, she had contacted her next door neighbour, a dentist named Dr. Seaman. She told him a man had stopped by her house enquiring about a car that Dr. Seaman was selling. The man had left a note with his name and phone number on.

The next morning, the dentist discovered Griffin dead in her home. She had a butcher's knife sticking out of her chest and her face had been smashed in with a toaster. A handwriting expert linked the note to Allen which linked him to the murder. He was quickly arrested and charged.

He was sentenced to death for all three of his victims but was later commuted to 60 years due to mental incapacity at the time of the murders. He is due to be released in 2035.

Active from 1974-1987. *USA.*

Victims: 3

19) Yuri Ivanov

A Soviet Union rapist and serial killer who raped and killed 16 girls and women over a 13 year period. From a young age he had developed a hate for women and if they belittled men then he would seek to kill them. He would mostly rape and then strangle his victims to death before taking some of their personal belongings as trophies.

He mostly killed in the mid to late 1970s. But in 1987 he killed a 16-year-old girl that led to his arrest because he returned to the crime scene. He confessed to the rape and murder of 16 girls and women, and another 14 rapes without murder.

He then identified all of his victims by photographs proving he had killed them all. In 1989, he was executed by firing squad.

Active from 1974-1987. *Soviet Union.*

Victims: 16

20) Gary Ridgway

Gary Ridgway, AKA: *The Green River Killer,* was an American serial killer who was convicted of 48 murders and has been linked to more since. He is one of the country's most prolific killers. He was active in

Washington State and killed teenage girls and women.

From 1982 to 1998, and possibly a little after, he had killed at least 71 people. In the early 1980s, the King County Sheriff's Office created the Green River Task Force to investigate the murders.

At his trial in 2003, he entered a plea bargain to plead guilty to 48 charges of murder instead of the seven he was originally charged with. This allowed the families of 41 more victims to find resolution. He claimed more murders and is linked to at least 71 in total. He was sentenced to life in prison and as of 2019 is currently incarcerated at the High Security Federal Prison in Florence, Colorado.

He is constantly being made available for information relating to open murder investigations. He remains one of the most notorious serial killers in the United States.

Active from 1982-2001. *USA.*

Victims: *49-71*

21) Lonnie David Franklin Jr.

He killed seven people from 1985 to 1988, but then came a 14 year gap when there were no killings. He then killed again three more times from 2002 to 2007. The gap between the killings earned him the notorious moniker of *The Grim Sleeper.*

Franklin would murder prostitutes, drug addicts and homeless runaways. He generally raped them before shooting them in the chest at close range. He then left their bodies in alleyways, in trash cans, or beside industrial bins. He knew the alleys well as he was a sanitation worker at the time.

In 2010, Franklin was arrested after the investigation had used familial DNA searching. Franklin's son had previously been arrested for gun and drug offences and his DNA was on the systems they searched. When they made the match, Franklin was found soon after and charged.

In June of 2016, Franklin was sentenced to death for 10 murders and one attempted murder. It has been suggested that he killed many more. He is currently on death row awaiting execution.

Active from 1985-2007. *USA.*

Victims: 10-25+

22) Robert Andrew Berdella Jr.

On June 23rd, 1987, *Robert Andrew Berdella Jr.* AKA: *The Kansas City Butcher,* dragged a sedated 20-year-old *Larry Wayne Pearson* into his basement. He would then violently torture Pearson for the next six weeks before beheading and dissecting his remains in August of 1987. Pearson was one of six victims to fall foul of one of the most evil killers in the modern era.

His first victim was in 1984. He promised to give a 19-year-old man named *Jerry Howell* a lift to a dance contest but instead drugged him with heavy sedatives, took him home and tied him to his bed. Over the next 24 hours, Berdella raped, tortured and beat Jerry. He died after the drugs stopped his heart and he gagged on his own vomit. Berdella then dragged the body to the basement to try and resuscitate him but instead he suspended the body from the feet.

As Jerry's body was hanging upside down, Berdella cut his throat and other arterial veins in order to drain the blood from the corpse. A day later he returned to his basement and used a chainsaw and knives to dismember the body. He wrapped them in newspapers and bags and put them in several trash bags where they were collected and taken to the landfill.

We know all this in such great detail because Berdella had been keeping extremely detailed notes and photographs of his victims and other assaults. Although Pearson was his last murder, another victim escaped his clutches in 1988.

22-year-old *Christopher Bryson* managed to escape from the house. He jumped from a second floor window and was wearing nothing except a dog collar around his neck. He broke his foot when he jumped but managed to call out for help. Someone heard him and called the police, resulting in Berdella's arrest.

334 Polaroid images and 34 snapshot prints were found in the apartment when it was searched. There was a possible link with a total of 20 murders but only six could be verified using his notes and confession.

He was sentenced to life in prison without parole but died of a heart failure on October 8th, 1992, while incarcerated at Missouri State Penitentiary.

Active from 1984-1988. *USA.*

Victims: 6

23) Timothy Wilson Spencer

AKA: *The Southside Strangler,* was a serial killer who operated in Virginia from 1984 to 1988. On November 22nd 1987, 15-year-old high school student Diane Cho, was found dead in her family's house, in

Chesterfield County. She had been raped and strangled by Spencer. He would be convicted of five murders from 1984 to 1987, and was the first serial killer in the United States to be convicted using DNA evidence.

His case also involved the first person to be found innocent of a crime they had previously been convicted for – all because of the advances in DNA technology. In 1984, Spencer claimed his first victim, Carolyn Hamm, from Virginia. Her body was discovered face down near the door to her garage. She had been raped, tied up and hung with a cord from a Venetian blind.

Her murder was in an area where violent crime was considered rare and due to media attention, an arrest was made quickly. A confession was obtained and charges were brought to David Vasquez who was wrongly convicted. He served five years of a 35 year prison sentence before becoming the first person to have his conviction overturned due to advancements in DNA technology.

Spencer was arrested in 1988 and subsequently convicted of murder and rape. He was sentenced to death and executed in the electric chair on April 27th 1994.

Active from 1984-1988. *USA.*

Victims: 5

24) The Frankford Slasher

The Frankford Slasher is a moniker for a serial killer who killed in and around the Frankford region of Philadelphia in Pennsylvania from 1985 to 1990. A black man named Leonard Christopher was convicted for one of the nine linked victims. He was convicted on minimal evidence and most witnesses saw the victims with a middle-aged white man before their deaths.

It has now been suggested that the murders are the work of an unidentified serial killer. All the victims were females of varying ages and had been raped before being stabbed to death. Almost all had been found half naked and positioned in a provocative position. Most had been stabbed multiple times and had been gutted.

Some bodies were found with their organs on display or their intestines spilled out. A kitchen knife used to kill one victim was left inside of her body. Leonard Christopher was convicted, even though there was no murder weapon, no reliable witnesses and only circumstantial evidence, he was sentenced to life in prison.

Two months earlier on September 6th, while Christopher was in prison awaiting trial, the body of 30-year-old Michelle Denher was found in her apartment. She had been killed in exactly the same fashion as the other victims but it didn't change the trial and Christopher was taken away to serve his sentence.

Investigators have since claimed there is no evidence that pointed to Christopher being The Frankford Slasher. The eight other murders are now part of an active cold case.

Leonard Christopher has since died of cancer.

Active from 1985-1990. *USA.*

Victims: 9

25) The Colonial Parkway Murders

Between 1986 and 1989, an unidentified serial killer was suspected of killing at least eight people along or nearby the Colonial Parkway of the United States Commonwealth of Virginia. Three couples were murdered and one couple went missing. It has also been suggested that another two people may have fallen victim to the same killer.

On September 22nd 1987, in Isle of Wight County, Virginia, 20-year-old David Knobling and 14-year-old Robin Edwards were found shot to death. The dating couple were discovered in the Ragged Island Wildlife Refuge, on the south shore of the James River. The two bodies were found by Knobling's father and a search party who were scouring the edges of the river.

Some other investigators believe the killings might have been someone in law enforcement. One investigator claimed that all the cars had their windows wound down and the only reason to have done it, was if they were being pulled over by an officer or ranger.

A deputy who was around at the time, named Fred Atwell, has constantly been mentioned as a person of interest. Most families of the victims stated that his obsession with the murders was unhealthy and he worked his way into their lives, too intimately to just be friendly. He was arrested in 2011 for robbing a woman at gunpoint.

As of 2019, The Colonial Parkway Murders have not been solved and remain a cold case investigation to this day.

Active from 1986-1989. *USA.*

Victims: *8-10*

26) Thierry Paulin

On November 25th 1987, French serial killer *Thierry Paulin* brutally murdered 79-year-old Rachel Cohen. She would become one of his 18 accused murders. Later on the same day he brutally attacked 87-year-old, Berthe Finalteri, but she would go on to survive and give a description that would result in the capture of Paulin. The killing of Genevieve Germont on November 27th 1987, would be his final victim.

Thierry Paulin had contracted HIV in the years prior and then AIDS. His killings sped up as he realised he was under a biological death sentence and set out to cause as much carnage and chaos as possible. He organised large and expensive parties that were all paid for with stolen credit cards along with the financial gains from his murders.

He was arrested on December 1st, 1987 and accused of the 18 murders. He confessed to 21 killings. Just over a month later, Paulin fell ill as AIDS set in. He was subsequently hospitalised and died on April 16th 1989.

Active from 1984-1987. *France.*

Victims: 18-21

27) Francis Heaulme

Francis Heaulme, AKA: The Criminal Backpacker, was a French serial killer. He had the rare condition of Klinefelter's syndrome, which meant he had a supplemental X chromosome, was infertile and had small testicles. In his formative years he was abused by his father and turned to drink before becoming suicidal.

At the age of 28-years-old, he left home to backpack around France, either by hitchhiking or cycling. Whatever money he earned was spent on drink and drugs. He would kill his victims with different methods and on random dates making his capture all the more difficult. He brazenly killed 44-year-old Aline Peres on a busy public beach in broad daylight, surrounded by people who witnessed nothing. Yet, it was this murder he was finally arrested for.

Among others, he murdered two children in 1986 and dumped their bodies alongside a railroad track in Montigny-lès-Metz. A man named Patrick Dils was convicted of the crime, and served 15 years in prison before being exonerated in 2002.

Heaulme was arrested in 1992 and went on to describe each murder scene in detail. He was sentenced to 22 years in May of 1997. Then he was subsequently sentenced to another 30 years in 2004 for three murders, and life imprisonment in 2017 for the murder of two boys.

As of 2019, he remains incarcerated.

Active from 1984-1992. *France.*

Victims: 9+

28) Michel Paul Fourniret

On December 11th 1987, 17-year-old *Isabelle Laville* becomes a victim of the *Ogre of the Ardennes*. French serial killer *Michel Paul Fourniret* confessed to killing 11 people in France and Belgium between 1987 and 2001. His wife, Monique Pierrette Olivier, was complicit in some of the murders and would be sentenced alongside him.

He was driving with his wife in two separate cars in a deliberate attempt to hunt their 17-year-old victim. They had spotted Isabelle a day earlier as she was walking home from school. They had set up a plan where Isabelle got into his wife's car to give directions, then they stopped at Fourniret's car which would appear to be broken down at the side of the road.

His wife then stopped her car and got out to see if he needed any help. When Isabelle approached as well, he raped and beat her before strangling her to death. They both then threw her body down a disused well. Fourniret was arrested in 2003 and confessed to killing eight females and one male. He was convicted of seven murders and sentenced to life. His wife was sentenced to 28 years

It wouldn't be until July 11th 2006, when Isabelle Laville's remains would be recovered.

Active from 1987-2001. *France and Belgium.*

Victims: *8-11+*

29) Pierre Chanal

French serial killing soldier Pierre Chanal murdered at least eight people between 1980 and 1988, although it is suspected he could have killed 17. The area of his killings became known as the *Triangle of Death*.

On August 8th 1987, the body of Irishman *Trevor O'Keeffe* was discovered in a shallow grave in France. He had been hitchhiking through the country when he was strangled to death by Chanal. At least eight young men had disappeared within the triangle since 1980.

In 1988, Chanal was stopped by police. When they opened his van doors, they discovered a Hungarian hitchhiker who had been tied and gagged. Chanal was convicted of kidnapping and rape but was suspected to have killed up to 17 people in the Mourmelon region of France.

His van was full of sex toys and a camera where he had been taking various images of men he had picked up. Astonishingly, Chanal was a Chief Warrant Officer in the 4th Dragoon Regiment in France. He had previously earned a United Nations medal for his service as a UN peacekeeper in Lebanon.

Pierre Chanal committed suicide in 2003 whilst on trial for the murders.

Active from 1980-1988. *France*.

Victims: 8-17+

30) Ismo Kullervo Junni

Born in 1943, Finnish serial killer Ismo Kullervo Junni would go on to murder five people from 1980 to 1988. Most of his crimes were committed at the Kivinokka summer camp area in Helsinki. He became known for removing his victims teeth.

Growing up he had witnessed his father killing his mother by stamping on her head and dragging her body to their bathtub. It was a traumatic experience that never left him. Throughout his formative years and in his adult life, he grew a bizarre interest in cadavers and would often visit mortuaries.

In August of 1980, Junni killed his wife and then pulled out her teeth. He was investigated but due to insufficient evidence the case was recorded as an accident. It wasn't until 1986 when he killed again. He killed two of his colleagues at the summer camp and then set fire to the crime scene in order to hide the evidence.

In July 1986, Junni killed his friend, Matti Haapanen, by smashing a glass bowl over his head, then he proceeded to set fire to his friend's summer home. Again in 1988, he killed another person by burning them alive in their holiday home. When Matti's wife reported Junni's strange behaviour of telling stories about the fire, he was arrested and charged.

He was convicted of four murders and also confessed to the murder of his wife.

Active from 1980-1988. *Finland.*

Victims: 5

31) Jukka Torsten Lindholm

Born in 1965 as Jukka Torsten Lindholm, the Finnish serial killer changed his name multiple times to be known as Michael Maria Pentholm and then Michael Penttilä. His crimes had started in his early life and showed no signs of letting up. When he was 16-years-old, in 1981, he abducted a 16-year-old girl and dragged her into a basement where he beat and choked her.

The girl escaped and identified Lindholm as the attacker. He was sent to a youth prison in 1984 for one year for various other attacks and thefts. In 1985, upon his release, he killed his 48-year-old mother in the apartment they shared. Despite being a suspect, he was not charged with the murder.

In July of 1986, he lured two 12-year-old girls to his apartment for alcohol. He locked one of the girls in the bathroom as he choked the other one to death. When he released the girl in the bathroom, he raped and beat her but she escaped and ran from the apartment. Lindholm was caught shortly after whilst hiding out in a forest.

On March 17th 1987, he was found guilty of two charges of manslaughter along with other crimes. He was sentenced to nine years in prison but was released on parole in 1992. He attacked more people in the year that followed, killed a 42-year-old woman, then escaped a police station in June of 1993. When he was recaptured, he was sentenced to another nine years in prison then sent to a psychiatric unit.

Astonishingly, he was released twice more in the years that followed, only to attack more women and kill again. His final victim was on April 13th 2018 when he killed a prostitute in a Helsinki apartment. Lindholm as Michael Penttilä was then sentenced to life in prison.

Presumably until he is released on parole again.

Active from 1985-2018. *Finland.*

Victims: *4+*

32) Robert Pickton

One of Canada's worst cases of serial killing began in 1983 and continued for 19 years until 2002. Robert Pickton, AKA: The Pig Farmer Killer, was responsible for at least 49 murders, even though he was only convicted on six of them. He was arrested in 2002 and charged with the deaths of another 20 women.

Forensic detection proved difficult because most of the bodies had either been decomposing for a long time or had been consumed by insects and pigs on the farm. The investigation included heavy industrial equipment such as 15-metre long conveyor belts and soil sifters, to find evidence of human remains.

In 2004, the Canadian Government confirmed that Pickton may have ground up human flesh and mixed it with pork to be sold to the public and to the wholesale trade. In conjunction with the Health Authority, they issued a warning about meat that had originated in the area.

Almost all of his victims were prostitutes from the Vancouver area. He was sentenced in 2010 to 25 years in prison without the possibility of parole, in what was the maximum sentence for murder under Canadian law. He confessed to 49 murders but wished to kill another to make it a round fifty.

During the trial, laboratory workers confirmed that 80 unidentified DNA profiles had been detected on the evidence provided to them.

Excavations at the farm continued for a year and cost upwards of $70million CAD. The area is now fenced off and all properties belonging to the farm have now been destroyed.

Active from 1983-2002. *Canada.*

Victims: 26-60+

33) William Patrick Fyfe

William Patrick Fyfe, AKA: The Killer Handyman is a Canadian serial killer convicted of the murders of five women in Montreal. He confessed to killing four more and killed his first victim when he was 24-years-old, in 1979.

He was arrested in December 1999 when DNA evidence on a door frame of a victim's house led police to him. He killed his victims by bludgeoning or stabbing them to death. He was convicted in 2000 and is now serving a life sentence at a psychiatric hospital in Saskatchewan.

Montreal Police also believe he was the serial rapist who had been referred to as *The Plumber*. The rapist carried out a large number of violent rapes throughout the 1980s in the Montreal area.

Active from 1979-1999. *Canada.*

Victims: 5-9+

34) Lindsey Robert Rose

On January 19th 1987, Australian serial killer *Lindsey Robert Rose* broke into a house in the West Ryde area of New South Wales. It was the home of *William Graf*, a known businessman. Rose had intended to rob the property of some of the more pricer belongings but he was caught in the act by Graf's partner *Reynette Holford*.

Rose then stabbed Reynette multiple times with a screwdriver and a vegetable knife. He tied her up after he had attacked her before running from the property, she was left to die of her injuries. Rose was caught ten years later in 1997 and was convicted of five murders over a 10 year period.

The first murder was in 1984, when he shot dead Edward John Cavanagh and Cavanagh's girlfriend, Carmelita Lee, in their home in Sydney.

He claimed it was out of revenge for Cavanagh beating up one of his friends a few years before. He killed Carmelita Lee as he did not want any witnesses to the murder.

As of 2019, he remains in prison serving five consecutive life sentences.

Active from 1984-1994. *Australia.*

Victims: *5*

35) Lainz Angels of Death

In Austria, a group of four women killed their patients over a six year period from 1983 to 1989. *Maria Gruber, Irene Leidolf, Stephanija Meyer,* and *Waltraud Wagner* were the four who made up the serial killing group.

They were nurse's aides at the *Geriatriezentrum am Wienerwald* in Lainz, Vienna. They killed their victims by administering overdoses of morphine or by forcing water into the lungs. Because elderly patients were prone to having liquid in their lungs, the murders were virtually unprovable.

The investigation claimed the hospital refused to help them when they looked at one of the deaths in 1988 and that they could have stopped more murders from taking place. The group were caught when a doctor heard them talking about their latest murder while they were out drinking in a local bar. When they were arrested they all confessed to a total of 49 murders. They were sentenced to between 15 years and life in prison.

By 2008, all four women had been released from prison and are supposed to be living in Austria under new identities.

Active from 1983-1989. *Austria.*

Victims: *49*

36) Michel Peiry

In Switzerland, Michel Peiry, AKA: the Sadist of Romont, killed 11 hitchhikers between 1981 and 1987. The Swiss serial killer is said to be the worst in the country since World War Two.

He would abduct or lure teenage hitchhikers then tie them up and rape or abuse them. Afterwards he would violently murder them and burn the corpses. In April of 1987, he claimed two victims. His ninth victim was on April 16th in the now popular Lake Como region of Italy. Eight days later, he attacked a young man in a similar fashion but the man survived. A week later, on May 1st 1987, Peiry was arrested.

Peiry was raised in an unhappy home and his father was violent to both him and his mother. He grew up to lead a relatively normal life until he began to repress his homosexuality. Out of this, he leaned towards violent sexual fantasies which he acquired through a love of bondage. He claimed that sexuality and violence became inseparable.

He was sentenced to life in prison, where he remains as of 2019.

Active from 1981-1987. *Switzerland.*

Victims: *5-11*

37) Denis Waxin

Waxin is a French serial killer and child molester who killed three young girls between 1985 and 1999. During that time period he would also rape another girl and two small boys.

Waxin's father was strict while his mother was hard-working and it is claimed the parents never spoke to each other. Waxin was neglected as a child and left alone in isolation, his only solace was his older brother who left the home when Denis was 17-years-old. He became depressed and walked the streets alone for hours at a time.

The same year, in 1985, Waxin lured seven-year-old Nathalie Hoareau to an area of wasteland. He raped and strangled her before stabbing her twice in the heart. Her partially nude body was discovered the same evening by police.

A few years later in 1990, he was confirmed to have killed nine-year-old Cathy Monchaux in Wazemmes. He lured her from her garden and took her to an old football field where he raped and then stabbed her 14 times. Her body was found the next day by a dog-walker.

In 1992, four-year-old Nadjia Thebib from Moulins went missing. Waxin lifted her up in his arms as her Aunt ran after him. The Aunt fell to the ground as she pursued him and lost sight of the direction he went in. Waxin raped Nadjia, stabbed her in the neck and choked her with a plastic bag.

On January 6th 1999, a six-year-old girl named Wendy was lured to an abandoned factory. He threatened her by telling her that he killed little girls and so she allowed Waxin to undress and rape her. He let her go and followed her to let her know he was watching her. A passing driver saw her and carried her to the police station.

The six-year-old girl gave a facial description to police which subsequently led to Waxin's arrest. He was sentenced to life in prison for the murders and rapes of children. He remains incarcerated as of 2019.

Active from 1985-1999. *France.*

Victims: *3+*

38) Horst David

German serial killer Horst David, killed at least seven people from 1975 to 1993. During his marriage from 1963 to 1984, he stayed away from the family as much as possible spending time in the cities of Munich and Hamburg. Due to his addiction with escorts and prostitutes, the family had financial difficulties.

The first murder in 1975 was a prostitute named Waltraud Frank. Just two days later, another prostitute named Fatima Grossart was found dead. David later claimed that he had argued with both victims because they had demanded more money than their standard rates. He divorced in 1984 and moved to Regensburg where he lived on state handouts. It was suspected that towards the late 1980s, he may have murdered more women. But it wasn't until 1993 that he would be linked to another murder. His neighbour, Mathilde Steindl, was strangled in her home.

His fingerprints were found in Steindl's dwelling but there was no other evidence linking him to the crime. In due course, his profile was sent to a new Automated Fingerprint Identification System (AFIS). It subsequently made a match with the fingerprints on Fatima Grossart's body from 1975.

Upon his arrest he confessed to a total of seven murders from 1975 to 1993. Three of the murders had never been investigated as murders because the crime scenes had been set up to look like household accidents. It is claimed that financial gain had been the sole motivation.

In 1995, David was sentenced to life imprisonment and remains incarcerated as of 2019.

Active from 1975-1993. *Germany.*

Victims: 7+

39) Thomas Holst

In Germany, on November 25th 1987, 21-year-old student *Andrea Grube-Nagel* goes missing. She was the first victim to be abducted and murdered by German serial killer *Thomas Holst, AKA: Heidemörder.*

As Andrea was leaving the Rissen Train Station in Hamburg, Holst had forced her into his car by putting a knife to her throat and threatening to stab her. He raped, tortured and dismembered her as he would his next two victims. Two days later, Andrea's remains were found by construction workers in the town of Kaltenkirchen, which is just north of Hamburg.

Over a two year period from November 1987 to November 1989, Thomas Holst abducted, raped and killed three women from Hamburg. Upon his arrest a psychiatric stated that he was '*untreatable and with extreme relapse probability*.' He was sent to trial for the violent murders of three victims and subsequently to a high-security wing of a psychiatric hospital.

Astonishingly, his therapist, *Tamar Segal*, helped him escape in 1995 as she had fallen in love with him. Holst gave himself up three months later and was detained at the Hamburg Detention Center where he has been ever since. In another bizarre twist, Thomas Holst married Segal while he was in prison in 1997 and by all accounts they are still married to this day.

Active from 1987-1989. *Germany.*

Victims: *3*

40) Lutz Reinstrom

German killer *Lutz Reinstrom,* AKA: *The Acid Killer,* murdered at least two people in his underground bunker from 1986 to 1988. He built the bunker in the grounds of his terraced house in Rahlstedt.

In 1986, he abducted a 61-year-old lady who was known to him as the wife of his teacher. He took her belongings and cleared her accounts. Then he raped, tortured and dismembered her over the course of a week.

The other known victim was in 1988 when he abducted a 31-year-old female. He emptied her bank accounts before raping and torturing her. The four-week torture was recorded by Reinstrom and he took multiple photos of her ordeal. He ended her life four weeks after her abduction by dismembering her.

He made his victims write farewell letters and postcards to their relatives stating they wanted to begin a new life in another country. Reinstrom would then travel to those countries and post the letters.

Another kidnapping in 1991 was botched when his wife came home from vacation early. He let his 53-year-old victim go and she became instrumental in his arrest. During the search of Reinstrom's property, five canisters of hydrochloric acid were found, along with a barrel full of human remains.

Active from 1986-1991. *Germany.*

Victims: 2+

212

41) Egidius Schiffer

German serial killer, *Leo Egidius Schiffer*, AKA: *The Strangler of Aachen*, killed five young women between 1983 and 1990. In Germany, his crimes became known as the *Disco-Murders* or *Hitchhiker Killings*.

He first killed in 1983 when he was 27-years-old. In Alsdorf, 18-year-old Marion Gerecht was waiting at a bus stop when Schiffer approached her and attacked her. She fought him and broke his windscreen but she was eventually strangled, stripped naked and her body was dumped in a fishing pond.

Then in 1984, Schiffer killed 15-year-old Andrea Wernicke after she was walking home alone from a nightclub. He raped her before strangling her and dumping her body near a dirt track. In the same year he murdered 17-year-old hitchhiker Angelika Sehl who was walking away from a different nightclub. Her partially clothed body was found in a forest shortly after.

In 1985, he abducted 18-year-old Marion Lauven from a bus stop, before raping and killing her. Schiffer drove across the country with Lauven's body in the trunk until he found a suitable forest to dump her corpse. It is unclear if Schiffer killed again before his next victim in 1990.

He was finally arrested in 2007 while he was trying to steal scrap metal. He voluntarily gave a saliva sample which was subsequently linked with five murders. He confessed to the five murders and claimed he received a massive amount of sexual pleasure in killing the girls. He was sentenced in 2008 to life in prison.

On July 22nd 2018, Schiffer was found dead in his cell.

He had been using electrical cables in a sexual manner and had accidentally electrocuted himself to death.

Active from 1983-1990. *Germany.*

Victims: 5+

42) Dimitris Vakrinos

On August 6th 1987, 43-year-old *Panayiotis Gaglias* was murdered by Greek serial killer Dimitris Vakrinos. Gaglias was a guest in Vakrino's house and had threatened to go to the police over a stolen shotgun. Vakrinos killed him as he slept in his bed by hitting him with an iron bar.

He moved the body and dumped it on the side of a highway not too far away from his home. The body was found eight days later. Between 1987 and 1996, Vakrinos was a taxi driver who murdered five people over minor instances of disagreement. He attempted to kill another seven, along with a raft of other crimes including arson and robbery.

Vakrinos was a serial killer who had a bad childhood which led to him associating with sexual oppression, low self-esteem and excessive anger. As he was shorter than the average man, he responded to challenges by using weapons in place of his smaller stature.

Vakrinos was caught and arrested in April of 1997. In May of the same year he committed suicide in the prison's shower rooms by tying shoelaces to the shower head.

Active from 1987-1995. *Greece.*

Victims: 5

43) Ahmad Suradji

In Indonesia, *Ahmad Suradji*, AKA: *The Black Magic Killer*, killed at least 42 young girls and women between 1986 and 1997. He became known by many names, including *Dukan AS, Nasib Kelewang, Datuk Maringgi*, or *The Sorcerer*.

Suradji's victims were between the ages of 11-years-old to 30-years-old and were part of an ongoing ritual that saw him needing 70 victims. He strangled them and buried them in the ground up to their waists, on his sugar cane plantation. He *planted* them in such a way that their heads were facing his house, believing it imbibed him with extra powers.

In 1986, Suradji's father visited him in a dream and commanded him to murder 70 females as part of a larger black magic ritual. Believing it to be a real commandment, he began his campaign of murder believing he would become even more powerful. Although he was linked to 42 murders, there were reports at the time that over 80 people had gone missing in the area and that he may have reached his target of 70.

On April 30th 1997, he was arrested after a rickshaw driver went to police after a body had been found, claiming he had dropped the victim off at Suradji's house. Suradji confessed to her murder and the murders of at least 42 other females in the same manner. When the investigation turned to excavating the sugar cane plantation, 42 bodies were found with some so far along the decomposition process that they could not all be identified.

He took his victims into the nearby sugar cane fields where he had them dig their own graves before burying them up to their waist. They believed it was all part of a magical healing ritual. When they couldn't move out of the mud, he then strangled them until they were dead and drank the saliva from their mouths. Then he removed the clothes of the victims and buried them back in the ground with their heads facing his house.

Suradji was sentenced to death and was executed by firing squad on July 10th 2008. He was allowed one last liaison with his convicted wife, Tumini, before he was led out to the firing range.

Active from 1986-1997. *Indonesia.*

Victims: *42+*

44) Wolfgang Abel and Marco Furlan

German-Italian serial killing duo, *Wolfgang Abel and Marco Furlan* were sentenced to 30 years each on February 10th 1987. They took part in the murders of at least 10 people from 1977 to 1984 in Germany, Italy and the Netherlands.

It was suggested that between them they may have claimed up to 28 victims. At each crime scene they left a leaflet, written in Italian, it showed a Nazi Eagle and swastika and each of them had a different slogan. *"We are the last of the Nazis"* and *"Death comes to those who betray the true god"* being two of them.

They were caught in 1984 and Furlan was subsequently released in 2010. Abel was released to house arrest and then finally released to live amongst us in 2016.

Active from 1977-1984. *Italy, Germany, Netherlands.*

Victims: *10-28*

45) Marco Bergamo

Italian serial killer *Marco Bergamo,* AKA: *The Monster of Bolzano,* murdered five women between 1985 and 1992. During his childhood he suffered from a stutter and skin disease that saw him be bullied by family and school pupils. In his teenage years he collected knives and always had a knife on his person.

At the age of 26-years-old, in 1992, he had surgery to remove one of his testicles. This combined with his isolation and social awkwardness was one of the reasons why he went on to kill.

15-year-old Marcella Casagrande was his first victim in 1985. She had been butchered by Bergamo in her own home and he had stabbed her multiple times. Six months later he murdered 41-year-old teacher, Anna Maria Cipolletti. She was known to have involved herself in prostitution to subsidise her teaching wage. She had been stabbed 19 times by Bergamo, but no sexual abuse had taken place.

From then on until 1992, another three prostitutes were killed. For one victim, he even left a note on her grave that said he was sorry for what he did. He was caught when his car was stopped by police who found bloodstains on his passenger seat and documents of the last victim in the trunk.

He was convicted of five murders and sentenced to life in prison. He died of natural causes in October of 2017.

Active from 1985-1992. *Italy.*

Victims: 5

46) Andrea Matteucci

Italian serial killer *Andrea Matteucci,* AKA*: The Monster of Aosta*, killed four people from 1980 to 1995. His childhood was marred with a criminal father who abandoned Andrea the year he was born. His mother was a prostitute who allowed him to watch her liaisons with clients. Andrea then grew a hatred of women who were paid to be with men.

He killed his first victim on April 30th 1980. He met a man at an abandoned Roman theatre but the man made sexual advances towards him and he killed him by stabbing him to death. From then on Matteucci grew a second hatred for people who have affairs or sexual contact with others while having a family of their own.

It remains unclear whether he killed anyone else before 1992 when his second confirmed victim was noted. Going against his own ideals, he met a prostitute named Daniela Zago. They argued about the money and Matteucci shot her in the head.

Two years later a Nigerian prostitute died at his hands, apparently over an argument relating to her '*unsatisfactory performance*'. He beat her before shooting her dead. He then proceeded to engage in necrophilic acts with her corpse before taking the body home and dissecting it with a kitchen knife.

All of his victims remains were burned which made the investigation difficult and it is also suggested that he may have killed more. On June 26th 1995, he was arrested in connection with the disappearance of his final victim. He confessed to all the murders and was sentenced to 28 years.

In March 2017 he was released from prison and sent to a psychiatric hospital. As of 2019, it is unclear whether Matteucci still remains there or has been released into the public domain.

Active from 1980-1995. *Italy.*

Victims: *4+*

47) Henryk Kukula

Polish serial killer Henryk Kukuła, AKA: the Monster from Chorzów, raped and murdered at least four children over a 10 year period from 1980 to 1990. He was only 14-years-old when he claimed his first victim.

During his childhood, Kukula showed signs of aggression towards people around him and was treated in a psychiatric hospital for suspected mental health issues. His mother allowed him to stop the medication and a year after he was discharged, he murdered a five-year-old girl then engaged in necrophilia with the body.

In 1984, he was sent to an educational facility where he beat a nine-year-old boy to death before having sex with the corpse afterwards. He was arrested and sentenced to 15 years in prison but was released only five years later. He claimed to have been raped multiple times by other inmates during his incarceration.

After his release in 1990, he raped and murdered two brothers aged five-years-old and seven-years-old. He was arrested again and sentenced to a further 25 years.

Astonishingly, Kukula is due to be released in 2020.

Active from 1980-1990. *Poland.*

Victims: *4*

48) Henryk Morus

Again, in Poland, serial killer Henryk Moruś, killed seven people in a six year period from 1986 to 1992. His first murder in 1986 was 60-year-old shop owner Teresa Grabowska, who was killed in her own shop.

He went on to kill another six people including a young couple in their home where the woman was pregnant, two more business owners, and a pensioner. According to those who knew Morus, he was a caring husband and a good man.

For four of the murders, he was sentenced to death. For the other three, he was sentenced to life along with other crimes.

He died in 2013 in a prison hospital when he was 70-years-old. Up until his death he had been a model inmate and had repeatedly apologised for his crimes. He died of a suspected heart attack and was buried by the prison as his family refused to have the corpse collected.

Active from 1986-1992. *Poland*.

Victims: *7*

49) Johannes Mashlane

South African serial killer Johannes Mashiane, AKA: The Beast of Atteridgeville, killed 13 people over a 12 year period from 1977 to 1989. His first victim in 1977 was his girlfriend who he strangled to death. He was sentenced to only five years and released in 1982.

From his release until his death in 1989, he raped and killed at least 12 small boys. He would either strangle them or stone them to death and would sodomise them before and after their deaths.

Mashiane was caught red-handed while molesting his 14th victim but police were informed and gave chase through a large Pretoria suburb. Before he could be caught he threw himself in front of a bus and was killed instantly. His suicide robbed the victims families of motive and justice.

Active from 1977-1989. *South Africa.*

Victims: 13+

50) Norman Simons

South African serial killer Norman Avzal Simons, killed at least 22 young boys between 1986 and 1994. He was convicted on one of the murders and is part of an ongoing court process to this day. By 1994, the residents of Mitchell's Plain were haunted by the plague of a serial killer known as The Station Strangler.

During his childhood, Simons was deemed to be an intelligent boy who played classical instruments such as the piano. He also learned and spoke seven languages and went on to a career in teaching. He taught Grade-five students, which is generally children aged between 10-years-old to 11-years-old. It is no surprise then that most of his victims were from that age group.

He is claimed to be South Africa's Andrei Chikatilo and was even inspired by the stories coming out of Russia. Chikatilo was a Russian serial killer who killed young boys and girls by mostly luring them away from train stations. Simons utilised the same method and thus became known as The Station Strangler. He is to this day, one of South Africa's most notorious serial killers.

Simons claimed that during his childhood, his older stepbrother raped him on many occasions during his formative years. His brother was an alcoholic Rastafarian who was murdered in 1991 in a separate incident. Simons also claimed that he heard his brother's voice in his head, ordering him to kill others.

He claimed his first victim in 1986 when he was just 19-years-old. He lured 14-year-old Jonathan Claasen away from Modderdam Station, before raping and killing him. Claasen's body was discovered on October 3rd 1986. Generally, Simons would tie their hands behind their backs and strangle them with their own underwear. He would dump the bodies near to the stations in shallow graves with the corpses laying face down.

On January 7th 1987, the body of 10-year-old Yussuf Hoffmann was discovered. He had been killed in the exact same manner. Hoffman had been raped and strangled to death with a piece of his own clothing. His hands were tied behind his back and his face had been pushed into the sand in the area of Rocklands.

On January 23rd 1987, the body of 13-year-old Mario Thomas was discovered in Kuilsriver, less than 20 miles away from the location of Hoffman's body. It was already becoming clear that a perverse serial killer was stalking the streets of Mitchell's Plain.

In June 1987, 12-year-old Freddie Cleaves was discovered near Belhar Train Station, just six miles away from the body of Mario Thomas. In August 1987, the body of 14-year-old Samuel Ngaba was discovered at the exact same station as Cleave's body.

On October 1st 1987, the seventh victim was discovered almost a year to the day of the discovery of the first victim. The unnamed boy was found in exactly the same location as Simons very first victim, at Modderdam Railway Station.

On April 13th 1994, Norman Simons was arrested in connection with another murdered boy who had been discovered on the now infamous Weltevrede Dunes, his dumping ground of choice.

He was sentenced to life for the murder of one of the victims but is claimed to have killed at least 21 more. He is currently incarcerated at the Drakenstein Maximum Correctional Facility in Paarl, the same prison were Nelson Mandela was imprisoned.

Active from 1986-1994. *South Africa.*

Victims: *22+*

51) Faye and Ray Copeland

American serial killing couple Faye Della Wilson Copeland and Ray Copeland killed at least five people at their farm between 1986 and 1989. They ended up becoming the oldest couple to be sentenced to death. Faye was 69-years-old and Ray was 76-years-old.

Ray was born in Oklahoma in 1914 and began life taking part in petty crime such as stealing livestock for financial gain. He spent a year in prison for his petty crimes and was released in 1940 when he met Faye, whom he married shortly after. It would be 46 years later that they would claim their first victim.

Before 1986, he had spent decades perfecting illegal money making methods which involved everything from scamming cattle auctions to not paying farm workers. He began employing drifters on his farm and used them to purchase cattle with bounced checks but when it didn't work the way he wanted it to, he moved up to murder.

In 1989, a previous drifter employee phoned the authorities through a crime stoppers phone number and claimed he had seen human bones and remains on the farm. He also stated that Ray Copeland had assaulted him with an attempt to murder him. The investigation firstly found three male bodies in a barn and then excavations unearthed further remains.

Faye was given four death sentences and life without parole. Ray was convicted of five counts of murder and sentenced to death but he died of natural causes in 1993 whilst on death row. In 1999, Faye's death sentence was commuted to life but following a stroke she was granted medical parole to a nursing home. She too died of natural causes, two days before Christmas Day in 2003.

It has been suggested that the couple may have killed up to 12 people on the farm.

Active from 1986-1989. *USA.*

Victims: *5-12*

52) Hadden Irving Clark

American murderer *Hadden Irving Clark,* AKA: *The Cross-dressing Cannibal* was suspected of being a serial killer. He is confirmed to have killed two people, one child and one adult but it has been suggested he killed more.

He had two brothers, one of whom was Bradfield Clark, he was convicted of killing and cannibalising his girlfriend. His only sister ran away from home as a teenager and later proclaimed that she didn't have a family.

Hadden already had a reputation for being evil. If anyone crossed him or dared to belittle him then he would kill their pets, sometimes leaving the decapitated bodies on their doorsteps. A doctor's report later divulged that Clark believed birds and squirrels spoke to him.

The first confirmed murder was on May 31st 1986. He killed a six-year-old girl named Michelle Dorr, who was a friend of his niece. He lured her to an upstairs room in his brother's house – the only brother to not be in prison. He pushed her to the floor and stabbed her in the throat. He then ate parts of her body before burying the girl in a bag, in a remote park nearby.

Cannibalism ran in the family. In 1984, after a night of heavy drinking and drugs, Hadden Clark's brother Bradfield Clark killed his short-term girlfriend Patricia Mak. He beat and strangled to her death and dragged the body to the bathtub. There he dissected her body, cooked her breasts on a barbecue and ate them. He confessed to his crime and was convicted of the murder.

After his arrest for the murder of a woman in 1992, he then confessed to murdering tens of women since 1974. In 1993, Clark was convicted of the woman's murder and sentenced to 30 years in prison. In 1999, after another trial, he was convicted of the murder of six-year-old Michelle Dorr and was sentenced to an additional 30 years in prison.

As of 2019, he remains incarcerated.

Active from 1986-1992. *USA.*

Victims: *2+*

53) Richard Angelo

On November 15th 1987, American medical serial killer *Richard Angelo* was arrested and taken into custody after assaulting a 73-year-old patient of his. By the time of his arrest, Angelo was only 25-years-old and had killed at least eight people.

Sometimes referred to as the *Angel of Death*, Angelo was a nurse at the Good Samaritan Hospital in the Suffolk County area of New York. He used poison to kill and was linked with at least ten deaths and the poisoning of at least 25 others. He poisoned his victims to bring on a cardiac arrest so that he could try and resuscitate them in front of other workers at the hospital. He claimed he did this in order to be seen as a hero.

Angelo was convicted in December 1989 for two of the murders, one manslaughter, and one criminally negligent homicide. In four other deaths he was convicted of associated assault. It is suspected that he killed at least 10 people.

Angelo was sentenced to 50 years in prison and currently remains incarcerated at the Great Meadow Correctional Facility in Washington County.

Active during 1987. *USA.*

Victims: *8-26*

54) Lowell Edwin Amos

Lowell Edwin Amos is a convicted murderer whose family members died under suspicious circumstances. The death of his mother and all three of his wives led him to be known as *The Black Widower*.

In 1996, he was convicted of the murder of his third wife, Roberta Mowery Amos. All the murders looked like accidents. He was convicted of premeditated murder, and murder using a toxic substance. One of his wives died after a hair-dryer landed in her bath water as she was in it.

Another died of a cocaine overdose after he injected a large amount of the drug into her vagina. After the death of his mother by apparent natural causes, he inherited over $1million USD. No autopsy was carried out due to her age but it is suspected he used sedatives to drug and kill her.

He is currently serving life without parole at the Muskegon Correctional Facility in Michigan.

Active from 1979-1994. *USA.*

Victims: 1-4

55) Bobby Jack Fowler

American rapist and serial killer Bobby Jack Fowler is suspected of killing over 20 people. Advancements in cold case investigation and DNA technology has linked him to a number of murders over a 23 year period from 1973 to 1996.

As part of the Royal Canadian Mounted Police E-Pana Investigations, there is DNA evidence that matches Bobby Jack Fowler to the murder of 16-year-old Colleen MacMillen, in August 1974. Her body was discovered in September 1974. She was last seen leaving her home to hitchhike to a nearby friend's house.

In November 1973, 19-year-old Pamela Darlington, vanished from

Kamloops while hitchhiking to a local bar. Her body was found the next day. It has long been suggested that she was a victim of Fowler's. In October 1973, 19-year-old Gale Weys vanished while hitchhiking from Clearwater to Kamloops. Her body was found in a ditch on Highway 5 just south of Clearwater. Her death was also linked to Fowler.

In 2012, the investigation used advancements in DNA technology to positively identify Fowler in the murder of MacMillen. The Royal Canadian Mounted Police strongly believe that he was responsible for at least 10 of the other victims on the list. However, many more murders took place after his arrest in 1995, when he was picked up on a rape charge.

As Fowler died in prison in 2006, the investigation of his suspected murders has been made more difficult. As of 2019, many of the cold cases remain an open investigation.

Active from 1973-1996. *USA.*

Victims: 1-20+

56) Gary Charles Evans

American serial killer Gary Charles Evans was a lifetime criminal who terrorised New York until his death in 1998. In October 1991, he spent two weeks on top of a building while he was working out the routine of a coin shop below. He then walked into the shop, asked for a valuation and then shot the shop owner in the head.

By 1993, he claimed he had already killed four people. His robbery skills were reaching epidemic levels. He stole almost 1000 items of antiques from a antique departmental store in Vermont, and then used an industrial crane to steal a bench from a cemetery.

In 1987, Evans managed to befriend David Berkowitz, AKA; The Son of Sam. Berkowitz from then on would refer to Evans as '*The Great Tricep King*', on account of his muscular appearance. It is claimed that on one occasion, Berkowitz had become angered by Evans as he had referred to him as '*David Berserk-o-witz*'.

Upon Evan's next arrest in 1998, he confessed to five murders and then led police to the resting places of his victims. Almost all of the victims had been dismembered. Shortly after, he escaped from a prison van. When police surrounded him, he committed suicide by jumping to his death from a bridge.

Active from 1985-1997. *USA.*

Victims: *5*

57) Donald Leroy Evans

American Donald Leroy Evans murdered at least three people from 1985 to 1991 but confessed to over 70 murders stretching back to 1977. He was born in 1957, the seventh of nine children. Their mother was a violent alcoholic who constantly beat her children.

By the time he dropped out of school, Evans was already involved in drug and gang culture. At the age of 16-years-old, he attempted to kill himself by mixing a combination of illegal drugs with cockroach poison. In 1986, he was convicted for the rape of a local woman and sentenced to 15 years in prison. He only served five and was released in 1991.

On August 1st 1991, Evans kidnapped a 10-year-old girl who he raped and strangled to death. He was arrested only four days later and confessed immediately. It had been suggested that the girl was alive during the rape and died shortly after of her wounds. For that particular crime he was sentenced to death.

He then confessed to more than 70 murders in 22 different States. At first, the investigation didn't believe him but some of the descriptions of his victims matched up to missing persons and he was convicted of another murder.

Evans was stabbed to death in 1999 by a fellow inmate, while in the showers of the Mississippi State Penitentiary. Whatever secrets he had, along with the true number of his victims, have now gone with him to the grave.

Active from 1977-1991. *USA.*

Victims: *3-70+*

58) Walter E. Ellis

American serial killer Walter E. Ellis, AKA: The Milwaukee North Side Strangler raped and strangled seven women in Milwaukee from 1986 to 2007. All seven of his victims were strangled by hand, with a rope, or with an item of clothing tied around their necks.

Upon his arrest in 2009, he refused to speak and remained silent until his death. Therefore the motivations of his killings remain unknown and he refused to cooperate with authorities and his own lawyers.

He was caught when his DNA matched semen samples found on six of his victims, and from a blood sample on a can of pepper spray at one of the crime scenes. He was sentenced to seven consecutive life sentences but died in 2013 from unknown natural causes.

Active from 1986-2007. *USA.*

Victims: *7*

59) Daniel Lee Corwin

On February 13th 1987, in California, 72-year-old Alice Martin was abducted by American serial killer Daniel Lee Corwin, whilst out walking near her home. Her body was found the next day in a field. She had been raped before being strangled and stabbed to death.

On July 10th 1987, in Texas, 26-year-old Debra Lynn Ewing was abducted at gunpoint by Corwin whilst working at the Vision Center in the city. Her body was discovered two days later in an undeveloped plot of land. She had been raped before being strangled and stabbed.

On Halloween 1987, Corwin stabbed to death 36-year-old Mary Carrell Risinger at a car wash. He had attempted to abduct her but she fought back and screamed for help. Corwin then stabbed her in the neck as her three-year-old daughter looked on from inside the car. She bled to death at the scene.

He killed three people, all in 1987, but the seeds were laid 12 years earlier. In 1975 when he was just 17-years-old, Corwin abducted a classmate from his high school. He bound her in his car, drove her to a remote area and raped her. Then he dragged her from the car, beat her and stabbed her in the heart. Miraculously, she survived and pulled herself to a road to get help.

Corwin was sentenced to forty years in prison but astonishingly paroled after just nine years of the sentence served. He was released in November of 1985 and then went on to kill only 16 months later. Corwin was subsequently convicted of three 1987 murders, sentenced to death and executed by lethal injection in December of 1988.

Active during 1987. *USA*

Victims: *3*

60) Phillip Carl Jablonski

An American serial killer convicted of killing five women in California and Utah. On July 16th 1978, he killed Linda Kimball, his former partner. She was stabbed, strangled and beaten to death. Prior to this he had met her in February of 1977 and lived with her before she gave birth to their daughter.

On July 6th 1978, he went to her mother's house with the intention of raping her. He didn't go through with it but the rest of the family found out. Kimball left him a few days later and he killed her on July 16th. He was arrested, convicted and released in 1990 to sate his bloodlust even more.

In 1991 he would kill his new wife and her mother along with two others. He would sexually assault all of his victims and either shoot or strangle them. In the case of Fathyma Vann, he had carved the words; '*I Love Jesus*', into her back. When her body was found, her eyes and ears were missing.

Some label Jablonski as a spree killer but his crimes and the sexual satisfaction he gained from them cannot be overlooked.

As of 2019, he remains on death row and shockingly accepts and replies to pen-pal letters.

Active from 1978-1991. *USA.*

Victims: 5

61) Michael Hughes

On December 1ˢᵗ 1987, in California, 30-year-old *Deborah Jackson* was murdered by serial killer *Michael Hughes*, AKA: the *Southside Slayer*. He killed seven females between the ages of 15-years-old to 38-years-old over a six year period from 1986 to his arrest in 1993.

He was first convicted in 1993 and given a life sentence without parole for the murders of four women who he had strangled to death. Then, due to advancements in DNA technology, Hughes was charged with further murders in 2008. He had raped and killed two more women and two more teenage girls during his active years.

One of the charges was later dropped as evidence wasn't as certain as the other murders, but it has still been attributed to him. Some of the confusion with the victims was due to the fact that another serial killer was operating in the same area. *Lonnie David Franklin Jr.* AKA: *The Grim Sleeper*, had left bodies in a similar fashion within the region.

Hughes was convicted in 2011 and sentenced to death. As of 2019, he is on death row at San Quentin State Prison.

Active from 1986-1993. *USA.*

Victims: *7+*

62) The Speed Freak Killers

The Speed Freak Killers is the moniker attributed to serial killing duo Loren Herzog and Wesley Shermantine. They were suspected to be involved in as many as 72 murders in California from 1984 to 1999. The pair disposed of bodies in old mine shafts, remote hills and many beneath a trailer park.

They were arrested separately in 1999, when they were both 33-years-old. Herzog was charged with the 1998 abduction and murder of 25-year-old Cyndi Vanderheiden, along with four other murders dating back to 1984.

Shermantine was also charged with her murder. Together they were convicted of the murder of two drifter killings in 1984. The investigation believed that Shermantine alone killed at least 20 people, with bodies scattered in old mine shafts and his own trailer park. Multiple witnesses testified against his character. Five women came forward and stated that he had violently raped and abused them.

Herzog and Shermantine were known to be involved in heavy amphetamine use, hence the moniker of the Speed Freak Killers. They killed for the thrill of killing and it was claimed that they also killed for sport.

In Linden, California, in February of 2010, investigators were led to a well where over 1000 bone fragments were unearthed. It took another two years for the well site to be excavated. The amount of bone fragments shocked even the most hardened investigators. Before more victims were found, Herzog killed himself while on parole in 2012, by hanging himself inside his trailer.

In 2018, the San Joaquin County Police Department re-opened the case of the Speed Freak Killers. In the hope that a new investigation with modern technology would link the killers to more bodies and give families of certain missing people a greater sense of closure.

As of 2019, Shermantine remains on death row at San Quentin State Prison.

Active from 1984-1999. *USA.*

Victims: *4-70+*

63) Gary Michael Heidnik

On January 2nd 1987, in Philadelphia, 23-year-old *Deborah Dudley* was kidnapped by rapist and murderer *Gary Michael Heidnik*. AKA: *Brother Bishop*. She was held captive and murdered on March 19th 1987. In less than six months from November 1986 to March 1987, Heidnik had kidnapped, tortured, and raped six African-American women.

During his childhood, Heidnik was emotionally abused by his father. He had long suffered with bed-wetting as he grew up and his father would punish him for it. He would humiliate his son by forcing him to hang his stained bedsheets from his bedroom window in full view of the passing public.

He would keep his victims prisoner in a pit in the basement of his home and would go on to kill two of them. Another victim, 24-year-old *Sandra Lindsay*, was kidnapped on December 3rd 1986 and killed in February 1987. She died of starvation and the effects of torture. He went on to dismember her body, cook her ribs in an oven, and boil her head.

It was suggested he may have minced the flesh, mixed it with dog food and fed it to his other victims but those reports remain uncorroborated. Heidnik was arrested on March 24th 1987, after a new captive managed to call for help. He was sentenced to death and executed by lethal injection in July 1999.

Active from 1986-1987. *USA*.

Victims: 3

64) Donald Harvey

On October 26th 1987, American medical serial killer *Donald Harvey, the Angel of Death*, was admitted to the Toledo Correctional Institution in Ohio. This was after being convicted in August 1987 of killing 37 people. Harvey was a hospital orderly who claimed to have murdered 87 people between 1970 and April 1987 when he was arrested.

Harvey had worked in the medical profession from the age of 18-years-old. When he worked at the Marymount Hospital in London, Kentucky, he claimed to have killed at least a dozen patients there alone. Harvey claimed that he initially killed his victims because they enraged him but then he insisted it was because he didn't want to see terminally ill patients suffering.

He killed by administering many different types of drugs, mostly whatever was available at the time. He used arsenic, cyanide, insulin or morphine. He even suffocated some of them or drip-fed them liquid tainted with HIV. Because he had worked in so many hospitals, his crimes didn't come to light for over 17 years. Investigators suspected he could have killed hundreds of people.

He was given 28 life sentences after pleading guilty in order to avoid the death penalty. In 2017, he was badly beaten in his cell and died of his injuries on March 30th of that year.

Active from 1970-1987. *USA*.

Victims: *37-87+*

65) Billy Richard Glaze

On August 31st 1987, American serial killer *Billy Richard Glaze* AKA: *Jesse Sitting Crow*, was arrested. Glaze was a suspect in the murders of three Native American women in the Minneapolis area at the time and was arrested while driving under the influence of alcohol. The officers found a bloody shirt and a crowbar in the car.

Evidence in hair samples taken from the crowbar were used to convict him of the three murders. Glaze was suspected of involvement in a possible 50 murders but with the evolution of DNA technology, Glaze's guilt has been brought into question.

It is suspected that he had no involvement in the crimes, as DNA evidence points to an unknown male in the murders, but a new investigation is ongoing.

Glaze died of lung cancer in prison in 2015, after spending 25 years inside.

Active from 1986-1987. *USA.*

Victims: *3-50+*

66) Joseph Roy Metheny

An American serial killer who is said to have killed 10 people but was charged on three counts of murder. He was an alcoholic and drug addict, as were most of his victims. He joined the U.S. Army in 1973 and claimed to have served in Vietnam although this was never substantiated.

He also claimed to have first killed in 1976 and was linked to more murders in the late 1970s. He would deliberately hunt women with drug or alcohol problems and in 1994 he killed a prostitute named Cathy Ann Magaziner.

He buried her body in a shallow grave and then returned six months later to dig up her corpse and remove the head. He unceremoniously threw the head in the trash. Her body would remain undiscovered for another year and a half.

In 1996, the decomposed body of Kimberly Spicer was discovered under a trailer just 10 feet from Metheny's own trailer. He would usually stab and strangle his victims to death. It is also said that he dismembered some of the bodies and stored the '*meat*' in his freezer.

Then he would mix the flesh with a combination of beef and pork to make burger patties. In the weekends that followed, he would sell the burgers on a small barbecue at the side of the road.

During his trial, he said he committed the murders because he enjoyed it and got a rush out of it, making him a prime example of a thrill killer. He also claimed he had no real excuse other than he liked killing. He was found dead in his cell in 2017.

Active from 1976-1995. *USA.*

Victims: *3-10+*

67) Anthony Kirkland

On May 20th 1987, Ohio serial killer, *Anthony Kirkland*, murdered his 27-year-old girlfriend, Leola Douglas. After killing her, he then set her body on fire. For her murder, he served 16 years in prison and was released in 2004.

In the five years after his release, he would go on to kill another four females. Including the aggravated murders and rapes of 14-year-old Casonya Crawford in 2006, and 13-year-old Esme Kenney in 2009, both of Cincinnati.

After various appeals and court proceedings, he was finally sentenced to death in 2018 and currently awaits his execution.

Active from 1987-2009. *USA.*

Victims: 5

68) Juan Segundo

On October 6th 1987, in Fort Worth, Texas, an unnamed woman awoke in the middle of a sexual attack by American serial killer *Juan Segundo.* He carried on the attack and then physically assaulted her before fleeing the property.

The unnamed victim survived the ordeal but at least four others died at the hands of Segundo. He was sentenced for the burglary of the house to 10 years in prison but was released only one year later. It wasn't until 2005 when he was arrested again by using DNA detection on cold cases.

He was sentenced to death for the 1986 rape and murder of 11-year-old *Vanessa Villa,* who he strangled to death. She was living in Fort Worth with her mother and siblings when she was killed. On that fateful Sunday, she went to help out at a Dallas flea market and returned home claiming that she wasn't hungry. It was unclear at this point whether Segundo had made contact with the girl whilst in the market.

That same night, Segundo broke into her home and raped her before strangling her to death. Segundo was known to be a family friend and was never suspected until DNA evidence linked him to the murder. It is also claimed that he even attended the funeral of the girl. Vanessa's mother even defended him when he became a suspect, informing the investigation that he was not the type to kill people.

He was also linked by DNA evidence to three more murders between 1994 and 1995. Segundo is currently on death row awaiting execution by lethal injection.

Active from 1986-1995. *USA.*

Victims: *4+*

69) Morris Solomon Jr.

On March 19th 1987, In Sacramento, the body of 18-year-old prostitute Maria Apodaca is discovered. She had been bound, wrapped up in bedding and then buried. She had been raped and killed by American serial killer, *Morris Solomon Jr. AKA: The Sacramento Slayer.*

Solomon had been raised in rural Georgia by an abusive grandmother. She would beat him and his brother daily if they wet the bed, spoke with bad grammar, or cried during a beating from the day before. There were times when she beat them for no other reason than it had become a normal routine.

She also made Solomon remove all his clothing and stand on a stool in the corner. She would beat his naked body until he bled, and on one occasion she tied him to a pole so he couldn't escape her violence, before whipping him with electrical cord.

On April 20th 1987, the body of 26-year-old prostitute and drug-user Cherie Washington was uncovered on Solomon's property. He had given police permission to search the car in his yard. Upon doing so they noticed a depression in the ground.

They borrowed a shovel, excavated the area themselves, and discovered Washington's body. She had been raped and killed by Solomon, before being bound, wrapped in bedding and then buried. This method became his modus operandi.

On April 22nd, Police discovered two more bodies on the property. 24-year-old Linda Vitela and 17-year-old Sheila Jacox were unearthed, they had been tied up and buried in bedding. Both victims were prostitutes and drug-users, and their bodies had been in the ground for a year before being uncovered.

On April 29th, another body was discovered on the property. 29-year-old Sharon Massey was discovered buried and wrapped in bedding near to the site of previous victim; Maria Apodaca. Massey had been raped and murdered by Solomon, and had been dead for approximately six months before her body was unearthed.

Solomon is currently on death row at San Quentin, after being convicted of six murders. He is linked to at least one more.

Active from 1986-1987. *USA.*

Victims: 7+

70) The Stoneman

In India, over a four year period, at least 13 homeless people were killed during their sleep. They were killed by an unidentified killer known only as The Stoneman.

The murders took place in Calcutta but at the same time, another 13 homeless people were killed in a similar fashion in Mumbai, two cities over 1,200 miles apart. The same moniker was also given to the Mumbai killer whose victims were killed during 1985 to 1988.

It has since been suggested that the killings were committed by the same person, which meant that The Stoneman was responsible for at least 26 murders. It still remains unclear why the homeless people were killed, or if they were murdered by one individual or a group.

The victims were all killed in the same fashion. The killer or killers found a homeless person sleeping alone in a dark area of the city. Then they would crush the victims head with a single stone that weighed as much as 30 kilograms. Almost all of the victims remain unidentified and it wasn't until the sixth murder that the police began to see the connections.

As of 2019, all the murders remain unsolved and no one has ever been linked with the killings.

Active from 1985-1989. *India.*

Victims: *13-26+*

71) Harrison Graham

American serial killer Harrison Graham was convicted of seven murders committed in 1986 but wasn't arrested until August 1987 when he was evicted because of the terrible smell coming from his apartment.

On August 17th 1987, in Pennsylvania, Graham was arrested and charged with the murders. He said he killed all of them while he was under the influence of drugs and mostly at the same time as having sex with the victims.

He kept the bodies of his victims in his apartment, wrapping them in bedding and piling them up in his bedroom. The bodies were found after an eviction notice was served due to bad smells coming from the apartment. He turned himself in after a week on the run, when his mother convinced him to.

Graham was arrested only months after another Philadelphia serial killer, Gary M. Heidnik, was arrested for similar crimes. A criminal justice professor named Anthony Walsh suggested that the lack of media attention to Graham's crimes was a media neglect of black serial killers in America. This was because people at the time didn't really believe black people were capable of serial killing. Except the 1980s saw a large number of black serial killers.

Graham was convicted of seven murders and sentenced to death which was later commuted to life after an appeal regarding his mental health. As of 2019, he resides at the State Correctional Institution Coal Township (SCI Coal Township) in Pennsylvania.

Active from 1986-1987. *USA.*

Victims: 7

72) Gwendolyn Graham & Catherine Wood

American medical serial killer couple Gwendolyn Gail Graham and Catherine May Wood killed five elderly patients Michigan, in 1987. They worked as nurse's aides at the Alpine Manor nursing home, where they killed all their victims.

They fell in love in 1986 when they both met at the nursing home. Graham had recently moved from Texas. Wood ended up testifying against Graham in order to gain a reduced plea but it has long been suspected that Wood was the mastermind and instigator of the murders.

In January 1987, an elderly victim was killed when the couple smothered her with a small towel. Until their arrest in 1988, the five deaths later attributed as murders, were considered to have been the result of natural causes. The first murder became a blood pact for the couple, which in effect prevented the other partner from leaving due to their joint guilt.

In 1987, a total of five elderly people were killed by the couple, most of the victims suffered from Alzheimer's. Wood portrayed Graham to be sexually and physically dominant and would turn the murders into a game. It was claimed that they took souvenirs from their victims but none were ever recovered.

They split up when Graham cheated on her with another nurse at the nursing home, before moving back to Texas. In 1988, Wood's ex-husband went to the police based on stories he'd heard Wood talking about. Both Graham and Wood were arrested and sent to trial.

Graham had secretly confessed to her new girlfriend, who testified against her. She was convicted of five murders and sentenced to five life sentences. As of 2019, Graham remains incarcerated in a Women's Correctional Facility in Michigan.

Wood was charged with second-degree murder and conspiracy to commit murder. She was sentenced to 20 years but has remained incarcerated. Wood is expected to be released in 2021. It is claimed that Wood was the mastermind behind all the murders and is a pathological liar who could manipulate people to do her bidding. One claim said that she had set up Graham in revenge for leaving her.

Active during 1987. *USA.*

Victims: 5

73) Steven Brian Pennell

American serial killer Steven Brian Pennell, AKA: The Route 40 Killer, killed five people in the State of Delaware. He is infamous for being Delaware's only known serial killer.

On November 29th 1987, Shirley Ellis was picked up by Pennell, with the promise of money for sex in his van. He then tied Ellis up, then brutally raped, beat and mutilated her. Her body was dumped near Route 40.

He victims mostly consisted of hitchhikers who he picked up in his work van along Route 40 in Delaware. The carpet of the van proved to be a vital piece of evidence in his capture, as small fibers from the carpet were found on the body of the first victim.

The carpet fibers were removed from the van by an undercover policewoman who was posing as a prostitute. She managed to pull some from it when she pretended to admire his carpet, before deciding not to go with him. While the fibers were being forensically tested, he was placed under surveillance.

He was arrested in 1988 and convicted of two murders. He pleaded no contest on three more murders on the condition that he be executed as a preference. There was another murder in 1988 that he was also linked to but not proven.

He stated that it would be easier to execute him rather than have his family see him in jail for the rest of his life. In 1992, Pennell was executed by lethal injection, the first to be executed in Delaware since 1946, almost 50 years after.

Active from 1987-1988. *USA.*

Victims: 5+

74) Michael Lee Lockhart

American Michael Lee Lockhart was a multi-state serial killer who became infamous for receiving three different death sentences in three different states. He had killed in Florida, Indiana, and Texas.

In Indiana on October 13th 1987, Lockhart killed 16-year-old Wendy Gallagher. He raped her and mutilated her before killing her. Her partially clothed body was discovered by her sister, in the bedroom of her family home. She had been stabbed four times in the neck and 17 times in the upper body.

A large pool of blood surrounded her body. As she had been so brutally murdered, her intestines were exposed and hanging out. Forensics turned up fingerprints that matched Lockhart's DNA.

In Florida, in January 1988, he killed 14-year-old schoolgirl Jennifer Colhouer in the same manner. He sexually assaulted her, mutilated her and left her body to be found by family. He was arrested shortly after and sentenced to death for each of three murders he committed.

"A lot of people view what is happening here as evil, but I want you to know that I found love and compassion here. The people who work here, I thank them for the kindness they have shown me and I deeply appreciate all that has been done for me by the people who work here. That's all, Warden, I'm ready."

Lockhart's final words – December 9th 1997.

Lockhart claimed to have killed dozens of people during his reign, across many states. He also shot dead a police officer who was trying to arrest him. Although convicted of three murders, it is unclear how many he might have killed.

Active from 1987-1988. *USA.*

Victims: 3+

75) Samuel Little

On July 13th 1987, American serial killer *Samuel Little*, killed *Carol Elford.* Her body was discovered on the streets of Los Angeles. DNA evidence has recently linked him to the murder and he is currently on trial for up to 60 more killings across the United States.

On September 3rd 1987, Little killed *Guadalupe Apodaca.* Her body was discovered on the streets of Los Angeles in the same way that Elford's body had been found. Recent DNA evidence has also linked him to this murder. He is suspected of eight murders in 1987 alone.

Samuel Little was in a homeless shelter in Kentucky when he was arrested in 2012 following DNA testing on various cold cases. He could be America's most prolific serial killer.

Active from 1970-2005. USA.

Victims: 34-90+

76) Robert Ben Rhoades

American serial killer Robert Ben Rhoades, AKA: The Truck Stop Killer, is suspected of killing at least 50 women. He was convicted of three murders and was due to be convicted of more until the victims families dropped the charges to save them the pain, and also because he had already been convicted on the others.

It is suggested that he raped, tortured and murdered more than 50 women over a 15 year period. The investigation arrived at the figure due to the routes his truck-driving job took him on, along with the correlations of missing people around the same time as he was in the location.

Rhoades had created a torture chamber in the sleeping area of his truck. He would keep women tied up in there for days and sometimes weeks, as he tortured and raped them before dumping their bodies. Upon his arrest in 1990, it was discovered he was heavily into the BDSM lifestyle and had been killing for at least 15 years.

He also took many photos of his victims. The most infamous is the disturbing photo of 14-year-old Regina Kay Walters, who was his last known victim. She had run away with her boyfriend before Rhoades picked them up. The investigation found that Rhoades had killed the boyfriend and kept Walters as his sex slave for up to a month before killing her. The last photo of her was only a few minutes before her death.

In 1994, he was convicted of the murder of Walters and sentenced to life without parole. In the past few years he has been extradited to various States across America to be charged in separate murder cases.

As of 2019, he remains incarcerated and is said to be assisting cold case investigators with missing persons cases.

Active from 1975-1990. *USA.*

Victims: *3-50+*

77) Angel Maturino Resendiz

Mexican serial killer and lifetime criminal Angel Maturino Reséndiz, AKA: The Railroad Killer, was suspected to have killed at least 23 people across Mexico and the United States between 1986 and 1999.

Most of the murders were committed near railway tracks, which is where he gained his moniker. He first killed in 1986 by shooting dead an unidentified female in Texas. He claimed that he killed her because she had disrespected him when he picked her up to join him on a road trip.

"Evil contained in human form, a creature without a soul, no conscience, no sense of remorse, no regard for the sanctity of human life."

From the wife of one of his victims. (2006).

On June 15th 1999, his final victims were killed. He robbed and ransacked a house near to a railway track in Illinois. There, he shot dead an 80-year-old man in the head. Later that day he beat to death a 52-year-old woman in the same area. Investigators later found the house owners vehicle 60 miles away, then found DNA linking Reséndiz to the murder.

He subsequently surrendered to police in July 1999 and was convicted of a murder that took place in 1998. He was sentenced to death and executed by lethal injection, in Texas, in 2006.

Active from 1986-1999. *USA, Mexico.*

Victims: *16-23+*

78) Andre Rand

Suspected American serial killer *Andre Rand, AKA: The Pied Piper of Staten Island*, kidnapped and killed children from 1972 to 1987. It is claimed that he kidnapped them to be used in Satanic rituals. He was convicted of the kidnapping and murder of a 12-year-old girl in 1987.

On July 9th 1987, 12-year-old Jennifer Schweiger went missing. After an intense and widespread search that lasted 35 days, her body was found in a shallow grave in an area of woodland. She had been raped and brutally killed.

Rand was arrested in August of 1987 and sentenced to 25 years to life in prison. Due to the statute of limitations, he couldn't be tried for the murder of his earlier victims and was due for release in 2008. However he was convicted on further kidnapping charges, which are not restricted by the statute.

As of 2019, he remains incarcerated and is now due for paroled release in 2037.

Active from 1972-1987. *USA.*

Victims: *1-5+*

79) Craig Chandler Price

On July 27th 1987, in Rhode Island, serial killer *Craig Chandler Price* claimed his first victim, and he was only 13-years-old at the time. He would be arrested before he even reached his 16th birthday, and by then he had already murdered four people.

On the evening of July 27th, he broke into a house only two doors away from his family home. He took a knife from the kitchen and killed the occupant; 27-year-old Rebecca Spencer, by stabbing her an astonishing 58 times. He would kill his victims usually when high on marijuana and LSD.

His murders were so violent that the handles would break off the knives with the blades still embedded in the victims. He killed one of his neighbour's eight-year-old daughter by crushing her skull and stabbing her over 30 times. He was arrested in 1989 when he was just 15-years-old, and sentenced to life in prison.

He continues to be violent in prison, having stabbed a prison officer in 2009 and another inmate in 2017. He has never shown any remorse for his crimes and remains incarcerated for at least another 25 years.

Active from 1987-1989. *USA.*

Victims: *4*

80) Chester Dewayne Turner

On March 9th 1987, in Los Angeles, 21-year-old *Diane Johnson* is murdered by American serial killer, Chester Dewayne Turner, AKA: The Southside Slayer. The victim was confirmed by DNA evidence provided by police, and he was finally arrested in 2003.

On October 29th 1987, 26-year-old Annette Ernest was found dead along the hard shoulder near Grand Avenue and 106th Street in Vermont Vista. She had been raped and strangled to death by Turner. He was sentenced to death in 2007 for the murder of Ernest and nine other women. Authorities believe he was tied to another seven killings.

In 2007, he was first convicted of killing 10 women from 1987 to 1998, in addition to the death of an unborn child. By 2014 he was convicted of another four murders, bringing his total to 15 victims, and linked to many more. He is suspected to be one of the most prolific serial killers in the city of Los Angeles.

He received death sentences in both trials. As of 2019, he remains on death row.

Active from 1987-1998. *USA.*

Victims: *15+*

81) Louis Craine

On January 25th 1987, 24-year-old Loretta Perry, was found dead in a housing block. She had been raped and murdered by serial killer *Louis Craine.* Craine was sentenced to death for Perry's killing and the killing of three other women.

On March 18th 1987, the body of Vivian Collins was found in an abandoned house in the 1600 block of East Century Boulevard in the neighbourhood of Watts. She had been killed and dumped in the same manner as Craine's previous victims.

On May 29th 1987, in Los Angeles, 29-year-old Carolyn Barney was found dead in a vacant lot near a housing project. Her body was found in the same block where Craine's parents lived. At around the same time, a number of black serial killers were active in the Los Angeles region and two of Louis Craine's murders were previously attributed to The Southside Slayer.

Almost all of the victims were young black women who were either prostitutes or drug users. The bodies would be dumped in remote parks, in alleys or in vacant buildings.

In 1989, Craine was arrested and sentenced to death for the murders of four women. He was acquitted in the trial of the fifth victim but it has since been attributed to him. Within months of being convicted he died of unknown natural causes.

Active from 1986-1987. *USA.*

Victims: 5

82) Joseph Michael Swango

American physician and serial killer Joseph Michael Swango is estimated to have killed at least 60 people through poisoning of patients and some of his colleagues. He admitted to four deaths but the investigation linked him to dozens more.

Swango joined the Marine Corps but received a discharge in 1976 for an unknown reason. He went to train at a medical school at Southern Illinois University School of Medicine (SIU). While there he went through a strict regime of physical training and was known to punish himself with push ups and jogging if he got something wrong.

From the moment he got a surgical internship, patients began mysteriously dying around him. He would kill by injecting them with drug overdoses. His crimes didn't stop at patients and he would drug his colleagues by preparing the food for them and lacing it with overdoses of sedatives.

By 1994, the medical community and an investigation was on to him so he changed his name and moved to Zimbabwe of all places. There he got a job in a hospital and continued to kill patients and colleagues. He was arrested in 1997 while boarding a flight to Saudi Arabia. First sentenced in Zimbabwe, he was subsequently extradited to the United States to be sentenced to three life terms with no parole.

As of 2019, he remains incarcerated at the ADX Florence supermax prison near Florence, Colorado.

Active from 1981-1997. *USA, Zimbabwe.*

Victims: *4-60+*

83) Charles Thurman Sinclair

On July 14th 1987, in Spokane, Washington, coin shop owner *Leo Cashatt* was shot dead and his coin shop was robbed. He was one of the victims of *Charles Thurman Sinclair*, AKA: *The Coin Shop Killer.*

Sinclair was an armed robber, murderer and rapist of women, and was active from the early 1980s. He left a trail of bodies across Western states of America and parts of Canada. Investigators followed his crimes across the country and he was arrested in August of 1990.

Police officers in Alaska arrested Sinclair for the suspected connection of eight murders. When the investigation searched a storage shed owned by him they found the evidence they needed. Maps, false ID machines, C-4 explosives, land-mines and an entire stash of rare coins were the tip of the iceberg.

He was subsequently linked to at least 11 murders and two rapes. He would specifically target coin shops to rob, before killing the owners to hide any witnesses. In October 1990, while in custody, he died of a heart attack, leaving the investigation at a standstill.

Active from 1980-1990. *USA.*

Victims: *11+*

84) Tommy Lynn Sells

On November 18th 1987, in Illinois, police descend on a mobile home in the village of Ina. Inside they find an entire family has been slaughtered. 29-year-old *Russell Keith Dardeen* was found in a nearby field he had been shot and his genitals were mutilated. His pregnant wife and son who were in the mobile home were beaten to death. *Ruby Elaine Dardeen* was so badly beaten that she went into labour. Shockingly, the newborn was also beaten to death.

Convicted serial killer *Tommy Lynn Sells* who was on death row for separate murders confessed to the killing of the Dardeen family. He had been convicted of two murders but was suspected of at least another 10.

His first killed in 1980, when he was just 15-years-old. He had broken into a house to discover an adult man performing oral sex on a little boy. Sells then killed the man in a haze of anger and violence.

His last murder was on New Year's Eve, 1999, in Del Rio, Texas. He lured and raped two small girls, 13-year-old Kaylene Harris and 10-year-old Krystal Surles. He stabbed to death Harris and cut the throat of Surles. Miraculously, Surles survived and stumbled 500 metres along a road to her house while holding her throat in place.

She then gave a description to the police and Sells was finally arrested just a few days later on January 2nd 2000. Surles went on to make a full recovery and was instrumental in the capture of one of America's most prolific serial killers.

Police connected Sells to at least 22 murders but he himself claimed over 70 victims. He was executed by lethal injection on April 3rd 2014.

Active from 1980-1999. *USA.*

Victims: *10-70+*

85) Serhiy Fedorovich Tkach

Over a 25 year period, from 1980 to 2005, Ukrainian serial killer *Serhiy Fedorovich Tkach* killed at least 37 women and girls. He confessed to over 100 more murders at his trial.

Tkach targeted young female victims between the ages of eight-years-old to 18-years-old. He would rape them before suffocating or strangling them. He would engage in sexual acts with their corpses, before leaving their bodies at random locations throughout the country.

In a chilling comparison with fellow Soviet serial killer, Andrei Chikatilo, Tkach chose victims near railway lines, especially those that had recently been installed. The tar of the tracks covered the scent of some of the bodies, meaning that police dogs were thrown off course.

In 2005, Tkach had the gumption to attend the funeral of one of his victims. It was other children at the funeral who raised the alarm as they had seen Tkach with the dead girl shortly before her abduction and death. He was arrested shortly after and confessed to over 100 murders.

In 2008, he was sentenced to life without parole for the murder of 37 victims. Ten years later on November 4th 2018, Tkach died of natural causes and was buried by prison staff. Thus bringing to an end the life of one of Ukraine's most notorious serial killers.

Active from 1980-2005. *Soviet Union, Ukraine.*

Victims: *37-100+*

86) Jose Antonio Rodriguez Vega

On August 6th 1987, in Santander, Spain, 82-year-old *Margarita González* was raped and suffocated by Spanish serial killer *José Antonio Rodríguez Vega*, AKA: *The Old Lady Killer*. He forced González to swallow her own false teeth.

Only two more victims were ever named after their deaths in 1988. The names of the other victims were never released publicly. Vega was diagnosed as a psychopath who would ensure he knew his victims routines inside out. He would then gain their trust until he was invited into their homes, where he would cold-heartedly kill them.

He also took souvenirs from each of his victims, including a television from one of them. Most of the murders were attributed to natural causes due to the age of the victims. It was only after his capture when police released a video of the items that Vega had collected. Other families then came forward claiming they belonged to deceased or missing family members.

Vega raped and killed at least 16 elderly women from the ages of 61-years-old to 93-years-old over a nine month period from 1987 to 1988. He was arrested in May 1988, convicted, and sentenced to 440 years in prison.

In October 2002 he was stabbed to death by two other prison inmates.

Active from 1987-1988. *Spain.*

Victims: 16+

87) Nikolai Arkadievich Dudin

On December 3rd 1987, Russian serial killer *Nikolai Arkadievich Dudin*, AKA: *The Grim Maniac*, shot dead his father. He hid the body for a year, when an arrest for rape saw him confess to the murder.

He was only 13-years-old when he killed his father. Due to his age he escaped the death sentence and was imprisoned, where he incited riots along with an attempted murder. He was released in 2000 and two years later killed at least another 12 people in various incidents. He would use guns, knifes and blunt objects to kill his victims.

During May of 2002 alone, he killed nine people in a month of terror. On the first two days of the month a young female disappeared, she was later found dead, having been killed by Dudin. On May 8th, he murdered an entire family, first by shooting the father dead and then the mother. Then he chased their 11-year-old daughter before stabbing her repeatedly until she died.

Two days later, on May 10th, he killed three more people in a triple murder, in what looked like a replication of the murders from May 8th. Just a few days afterwards, he killed two more people in a double murder.

In July 2002, he was caught red-handed attempting to kill someone. He was arrested and sentenced to life imprisonment without parole. He was subsequently sent to a special regime colony; the *Supermax White Swan Prison*, where he remains to this day.

Active from 1987-2002. *Russia*.

Victims: 13

88) Francisco Garcia Escalero

Spanish serial killer Francisco García Escalero was convicted for the murders of 11 people over a seven year period from 1987 to 1994. He was a diagnosed schizophrenic who had sex with his victims corpses and engaged in cannibalism.

He claimed his first victim in August of 1987, a prostitute by the name of Paula Martínez. He stated he killed people because the voices in his head told him to, and his hallucinations caused by schizophrenia forced him to kill. He raped, killed and decapitated Martínez before burning her corpse.

In the years that followed he killed lots of homeless people and beggars. Sometimes he stabbed them to death and other times he crushed their skulls with rocks. The burned bodies of some victims were found decapitated. Alongside the murders he would go to local cemeteries and dig up bodies so he could have sex with them. He was also known to have eaten parts of the corpses.

He was arrested after escaping from a psychiatric hospital that he was in temporarily. Escalero attempted suicide but was stopped in the process. He confessed and was sent to trial in 1995. At the trial he was declared insane and sentenced to a life term at a high-security psychiatric hospital.

Active from 1987-1994. *Spain.*

Victims: 11

89) Michael Wayne McGray

Canadian serial killer Michael Wayne McGray was convicted of killing seven people but claimed to have killed 11 more. He killed over a 14 year period between 1984 and 1998.

The first murder was in May of 1985 when McGray was only 19-years-old. He picked up a 17-year-old hitchhiker named Elizabeth Gale Tucker then drove her to a remote wooded area in Nova Scotia, where he brutally killed her and dumped the body in a shallow grave.

On November 14th 1987, McGray robbed a taxi driver with two newfound accomplices. It is claimed that McGray killed the driver, but evidence was thin. A trial for one of his accomplices, Norm Warren, ended with a not-guilty verdict. McGray was however sentenced to five years for the robbery and couldn't be charged in the taxi driver's death.

On March 30th 1991, he was given a three-day parole pass to a halfway house in Montreal. During those three days, McGray killed three more people and then returned to prison over a month late. The day he was paroled he was invited back to a gay man's house where McGray stabbed him multiple times in the throat and chest.

A day later on March 31st, he went back to a gay meeting area and was invited back to another man's house. He stayed the night before waking up and stabbing the man to death. A day later he killed another gay man, which meant he had killed three victims in three days.

Upon his release he went on to kill many more. More confirmed victims came in 1998 when he killed a mother and daughter in their apartment. Joan Hicks and her 11-year-old daughter Nina were living in New Brunswick when McGray broke into their home. Joan was beaten to death and her throat had been cut. Nina was discovered in her bedroom closet, hanging from her neck.

The next day he was arrested and confessed to all the murders and more. He claimed 11 victims across the entirety of Canada and one in Seattle. He said if he was ever released that he would kill again. While in prison he killed another inmate and was transferred to a high security prison to live out the rest of his life sentence without parole.

In Nova Scotia on July 12th 2019, cold case investigators confirmed another female victim from 1995. Shockingly, her boyfriend had been convicted and spent 17 years in jail for a crime he didn't commit.

That case is now active and ongoing.

Active from 1984-1998. *Canada.*

Victims: *7-18+*

90) Andras Pandy

The Belgian-Hungarian serial killer *András Pándy,* AKA: *Father Bluebeard* was convicted for the murder of six family members in Brussels between 1986 and 1990. He has since been linked to at least another eight murders. His two former wives and two children disappeared mysteriously and it has long been suspected that Pandy had killed them and disposed of the bodies.

It is claimed that he killed them all with the help of another daughter named Agnes. He had been involved in a violent incestuous relationship with Agnes since she was a youngster and it had continued into adulthood. In 1984, he began another incestuous relationship with another of his daughters and had Agnes beat her in the basement when she didn't comply. The other girl later escaped to live a new life elsewhere in Hungary.

From 1986 to 1990, multiple children of both his daughter's also disappeared, when family members returned from holiday, Pandy told them their siblings had gone to live elsewhere. In reality, Pandy had killed them and disposed of their bodies.

In 1997, both Pandy and Ágnes were arrested. It was the confession of Ágnes that sealed both their fates. She claimed she had helped her father kill most of her disappeared relatives, but was solely complicit in the murder of her own mother. They both killed the family members by shooting or hitting them in the head with a sledgehammer.

The bodies were cut into pieces and taken to a bathtub in the basement of their home where they dissolved them with acid and other chemicals. Any remaining bones were taken to a local slaughterhouse for disposal.

In 2002, Pandy was convicted of six murders and the rape of three of his daughters, and sentenced to life without parole. Ágnes was sentenced to 21 years for being an accomplice in five murders and one attempted murder. She later claimed to be completely under her father's control and had no way to get out of the situation she found herself in.

In 2013 András Pándy died from natural causes in a Bruges prison. As of 2019, Ágnes remains incarcerated awaiting parole.

Active from 1986-1990. *Belgium.*

Victims: *6-14+*

91) Adolfo Constanzo

American serial killer and cult leader *Adolfo de Jesús Constanzo* was responsible for the deaths of numerous people through ritualistic killings with members of his cult.

He was also a drug dealer and ran a cult named The Narcosatanists. He was nicknamed the Godfather by his disciples and took part in multiple murders within Mexico. By 1987, Constanzo had started to believe that his magic was responsible for the success of the Mexican drug cartels and wished to be a business partner to a crime syndicate known as The Calzadas.

When they rejected his wishes, seven members of the Calzadas family were brutally murdered. They were found later with body parts missing. Most of them had their brain removed and one had his entire spine ripped out. The spinal column was never discovered.

In 1988, he moved the cult to a ranch in the Mexican desert where together they carried out more ritual murders. They started killing drifters and other rival drug dealers. On March 13th 1989, cult members abducted an American student from a Mexican bar. Mark Kilroy was taken back to the ranch where Constanzo killed him in front of his cult.

The American authorities pressured the Mexican Police to get answers on Kilroy's disappearance. The investigation led to Constanzo and the infamous ranch, where 15 mutilated corpses were unearthed. They also discovered a ritualistic cauldron which contained dead black cats and human brains.

Constanzo died in a firefight with Mexican Police when he had fled to Mexico City with some of the cult. A total of 14 other cult members were subsequently sentenced to 60 years each. Most are still incarcerated to this day.

Active from 1986-1989. *Mexico.*

Victims: *1-15+*

92) Hwaseong Serial Murders

On January 10th 1987, in South Korea, 19-year-old *Hong Jin-young* is found murdered. She is a victim of the unsolved *Hwaseong Serial Murders*. At least 10 females between the age of 14-years-old to 71-years-old were found tied, raped and strangled with their own clothing. The murders took place between 1986 and 1991 and remain unsolved to this day.

On May 2nd 1987, the body of 29-year-old *Park Eun-joo* is discovered. She too had been tied, raped and strangled with her own clothing. The killings are one of South Korea's most notorious unsolved crimes.

Serial killing is rare in South Korea, or at the least not brought into the public eye. This is one of the only cases where a killer using the same modus operandi had been identified in the country. Because of the outdated notion of *statute of limitations*, the killings could not be investigated after 2006. Police still keep records due to the infamy of the case.

Statute of limitation means that there is a maximum time limit placed on crimes for when legal proceedings can be brought to an individual. Many Western countries have a statute of limitations in place. The United Kingdom is the exception in that there is no current time limit in place.

A list of over 21,000 suspects has been put together over the years but as of 2019, the murders remain a mystery.

Active from 1986-1991. *South Korea.*

Victims: 10+

93) El Psicopata (The Psychopath)

On July 14th 1987, prostitute *Ligia Camacho Bermudez* was murdered in her home as she was laying on her bed reading a book. She had been shot from outside her house, through the window.

When ballistics were run, it showed the murder was carried out by a notorious Costa Rican serial killer known as *The Psychopath* (El Psícopata). Between 1986 and 1996, The Psychopath was responsible for the murders of at least 19 people in major cities across the country.

The last known murders of El Psícopata were on October 26th 1996. A young couple were parked beside a road near San José. The killer forced them at gunpoint to get out and leave their car behind, he then marched them away from the road and shot them both in the head. It was never clear what happened to the killer after the final murders.

In 1996, the suspect was identified by the Civil Police but never found. Due to the Costa Rican statute of limitations having passed, even if a suspect was found today, he could not be tried for the murders. This effectively means that the culprit would get off scot-free.

Active from 1986-1996. *Costa Rica.*

Victims: 19+

94) Richard Gladwell McGown

Richard Gladwell McGown was a Scottish-Zimbabwean murderer and suspected medical serial killer. He was convicted of the murders of two children from 1986 to 1992 but had been linked to at least three more. He had injected an overdose of morphine into their bloodstream which killed them within minutes.

Back in 1981, McGown had started to hold his own medical experiments to test new drugs and anaesthetics. He did this in Zimbabwe where he had been settled since the 1960s. Without the knowledge of his patients he is said to have experimented on at least 500 Zimbabwean children. Some of those children would later die from his experiments.

He was arrested in 1993 and an investigation into his conduct took place. A group of Zimbabwean students turned up outside the court and threatened to kill white people if the doctor wasn't sentenced. The case caused uproar in the country and a lead prosecutor stated that McGown was a '*messenger of death stalking our hospitals.*' He was charged with five murders but convicted of only two. It was unclear why the other charges were dropped. McGown was referred to as a Nazi and a racist by Zimbabwean media and the general public.

Despite being convicted for two murders, he was only sentenced to one year in prison which was reduced to six months because of a suspended sentence. He was told to pay $1,250 USD to the families of the victims. The families called the case and sentence a mockery of justice.

After his release, he returned to the United Kingdom and even went as far as appealing his medical license in a British Court. The British

General Medical Court banned him from entering a medical profession or practising medicine anywhere in the world.

Since 1995, Richard McGown has been free to live among us.

As of 2019, his whereabouts remain unknown.

Active from 1986-1992. *Zimbabwe.*

Victims: 5+

95) Naceur Damergi

Tunisian serial killer Naceur Damergi raped and killed 13 children in the Nabeul region of the country over a four year period from 1984 to 1988. Damergi had been born in prison to his prostitute mother and didn't meet his father until he was 30-years-old.

When he was 16-years-old, in 1960, he got engaged to his cousin then worked in France to raise money for the marriage. When he permanently returned in 1968, he found out that his cousin had married another man without telling him. It had enraged him so much so that in 1970 he raped a 12-year-old girl and then tried to kill the girl's sister.

He was sentenced in 1971 for the rape and attempted murder and wouldn't be released until 1984. During the time in prison he had built up an unhealthy image of children, and over the following four years he raped and murdered 13 young girls.

In 1988 he was sentenced to death for the rapes and murders. He was hanged on November 17th 1990, and remains one of Tunisia's worst serial killers.

Active from 1984-1988. *Tunisia.*

Victims: 13

96) Dennis Rader

In Wichita, American serial killer *Dennis Lynn Rader,* AKA: *The BTK Killer,* murdered at least 10 people between 1974 to 1991. BTK stood for Bind, Torture, Kill, and it was a moniker that Rader gave himself in letters to police and media.

The first confirmed murders were in 1974 when Rader killed four family members. Joseph Otero, Julie Otero and their two young children were brutally murdered in their own home. Their eldest son, Charlie Otero, returned home to find his family dead.

Rader had a habit of writing letters to the police investigating his murders, along with the newspapers. He would taunt them and refer to himself under various monikers, one of which; The BTK Killer, he became known for.

In 1985, a particularly brutal murder took place. On April 17th, he killed 53-year-old Marine Hedge. He killed her under his own murder codename of *Project Cookie,* and it was clear he had planned her death for many weeks. He took her corpse to a church and positioned her nude body in various BDSM positions. He then took numerous photographs of her before dumping the body in a ditch.

The last murder was in February 1991 when he killed an elderly lady, before dumping her body on the side of the street. He wrote letters to the police describing how he did it. Then a decade passed with apparently no killings and because he had passed from the public eye he started sending letters again in 2004.

By that time the BTK killings had become a cold case and it was Rader's desire to be infamous that saw him caught. In one letter he brazenly asked if a floppy disk could be traced if he sent one to them with images and writings. The police answered in a newspaper ad that it could not be traced. Rader believed them and sent a floppy disk to the investigators.

Police found metadata on a deleted word document. The information it contained led them to Rader. He had sealed his own fate by giving too much information to the police in the belief that he was untouchable. He was arrested shortly after and subsequently convicted of ten murders.

As of 2019, he is serving 10 life sentences at the El Dorado Correctional Facility in Kansas.

Active from 1974-1991. *USA.*

Victims: 10

97) Robert Joseph Silveria Jr.

American serial killer *Robert Joseph Silveria Jr.* AKA: *The Boxcar Killer,* murdered between nine and 28 victims. Over a period of 15 years from 1981 to 1996, Silveria rode the freight train routes and claimed to have killed 28 people.

Silveria was part of the Freight Train Riders of America (FTRA) who were suspected to be a criminal group that committed crimes by moving between freight trains all over the United States and Canada. Some of them were thought to have been involved in train derailments.

The FTRA was claimed to have been created by a group of Vietnam War veterans who were distraught at their treatment by the United States government. They slept in box cars, under bridges, and in train yards.

Silveria was linked to the murders of homeless people and runaways along the freight rail routes. He would shoot or stab them before leaving their bodies in the open. He was also known as '*Boxcar Bob*'. Because of these murders, the FTRA received nationwide attention and a large investigation began.

Another FTRA member, named Michael Elijah Adams, was also eventually caught and linked to 17 murders. Another recent FTRA member, Robert James LeCou, was convicted of killing three people in Montana, he was subsequently sentenced to 300 years in prison.

Silveria was arrested in 1996 and was sentenced to double life sentences without parole. He was also convicted in Wyoming, Florida, and Kansas, but remains imprisoned in a Medium Correctional Institution in Wyoming.

Active from 1981-1996. *USA.*

Victims: 9-28

98) David Parker Ray

American serial killer and torturer David Parker Ray, AKA: The Toy-Box Killer was suspected to have killed up to 60 people. Astonishingly no bodies have ever been found. Witness statements combined with missing persons reports, assured police that Ray was potentially one of America's worst serial killers.

He soundproofed and kitted out a truck trailer with instruments of torture and sexual devices, and called it his *toy box*. By the end of the trial in 2001, Ray had been convicted of kidnapping and torture but was never convicted of murder.

However, since then using advancements in DNA technology and investigatory procedures he has been positively linked to 14 murders.

The town he lived in was called Elephant Butte which is a small town in New Mexico. He had positioned the toy box trailer in one location for many years, it just so happened to be next to a large lake and a large New Mexico area of parkland. It has been suggested that bodies would have been easy to dump in the area, due to its remoteness. The area has never been excavated.

Ray also had extensive knowledge of the region as he worked as a maintenance man for the New Mexico Parks Department. It is claimed that his knowledge of the land allowed him to hide bodies all over the place. He would sexually torture his victims by using sexual instruments and industrial items. These included saws, blades, straps, clamps, whips and chains. He also had multiple accomplices, some of whom have never been named. Together they raped tens of women.

He also kept detailed illustrations regarding his various techniques for torture and restraint. He even had an electrical generator he used to torture his victims. He also put them in large contraptions that kept them bent over in one position, placed a mirror in front of them, and brought in dogs in to rape them.

Ray kept a detailed journal which contained information on his victims with dates of abductions and murders. It is claimed that without it, there wouldn't have been any prosecution. However, the FBI had built up a large case against him and three trials took place for the kidnap and torture of three victims. He was subsequently sentenced to 224 years.

In 2002, as part of his plea agreement, he agreed to show investigators where the bodies were buried. Just before he was about to, he died of a heart attack. In doing so, he took the locations of the bodies to his grave.

As of 2019, no bodies have ever been discovered.

Active from *mid*-1950s-1999. *USA.*

Victims: *14-60+*

99) Robert Black

Scottish serial killer, Robert Black, was convicted in 1994 for the rapes and murders of four young girls in the United Kingdom. It is known he killed eight children across Europe and was suspected in 13 more. Black was a paedophile and killer who operated from 1969 to 1987.

He was a truck driver who made regular work trips to mainland Europe where it is suspected he murdered dozens more. He was also prime suspect in the infamous 1978 disappearance and murder of 13-year-old Genette Tate. She had vanished one day on her newspaper delivery round, in Devon on England's Southern Coast.

Ray was born in Grangemouth, Scotland, in 1947. Because his mother didn't know who the father was, she had Black adopted, and he lived with a couple in Kinlochleven, in the Scottish Highlands. He went through life, known with the surname of Tulip, which he took from his adopted parents.

When he was 11-years-old, both his foster parents died from apparent natural causes and he was adopted by another couple in the small village. There, he dragged a younger girl into a public toilet and attempted to rape her. His new foster parents had him removed from their care to a mixed-sex children's care home near Falkirk on the central belt of Scotland.

He abused girls there and was sent to a stricter care home for boys only. It was there that he was abused by a male carer for up to three years. He would regularly be forced to perform oral sex on the carer. In 1963, he lured a seven-year-old girl to an abandoned air-raid shelter. He throttled her until she passed out then he masturbated over her body. Ray was only 16-years-old at the time.

His first confirmed murder victim was in August of 1981, when he abducted nine-year-old Jennifer Cardy in Northern Ireland, while on a long-haul journey. She had been riding her bike near to a main road when she vanished. Hundreds of volunteers joined the search for the girl and her body was found in a large lake, six days later by two fisherman. Black had raped and drowned the girl.

Along with multiple disappearances and murders in the United Kingdom, there were also connections to disappearances across Ireland, the Netherlands, France and Germany. All of the victims vanished or were killed at the same time as Black would have been in the areas on his long-haul European journeys.

The nationwide manhunt for Robert Black was one of the most expensive UK murder investigations of the 20th Century. He was arrested for attempting to abduct a girl in 1990.

In 1994 he was convicted of the rape and murder of three girls, along with kidnapping and sexual assault. He received a sentence of life imprisonment with a minimum of 35 years.

Robert Black remains one of the worst serial killers to have walked the streets of the United Kingdom and Europe. He died of a heart attack in 2016.

Active from 1969-1990. *UK.*

Victims: *4-21+*

100) Vincent Darrell Groves

On July 4th 1987, 18-year-old Karolyn Walker, was brutally murdered in Aurora by American serial killer *Vincent Darrell Groves*. Her body was found a day later. Upon his second capture in 1988, Groves was suspected of killing 17 prostitutes over a 10 year period from 1978 to 1988.

This was despite being in prison on a five year term for second degree murder from 1982 to 1987. Almost immediately upon his release, he began to kill again with three bodies discovered in 1987 alone. He would eventually be convicted on two more counts of murder.

He was sentenced to life for murder In 1996, while investigations were still continuing, Groves died in prison, leaving behind a dark legacy that affected many lives.

Active from 1978-1988. *USA.*

Victims: *14-17+*

Appendices

The following sections include extra segments that are relevant to the content of *1987: Year of the Serial Killer, Chapter Two*. There's also an extensive bibliography which has information on the studies, statistics and various data cited and referenced in this book.

Three of the appendices at the back of the book are small segments that were also available in *1978: Year of the Serial Killer.* They have been added in addition, due to their relevancy regarding 1987.

(I) Rise of the Highway Killer

In 1978: Year of the Serial Killer, there was a lot of discussion and points made about the construction of the highways and interstates which led to a rise in serial killing. There were a number of killers who took advantage of it in 1978 and in 1987.

In fact more serial killers were dumping bodies alongside highways in 1987 than they were in 1978. Project E-PANA was one of the biggest investigations. It was created in 2005 to review and investigate numerous unsolved murders on Highway 16, which became known as the Highway of Tears. It was created by the Royal Canadian Mounted Police (RCMP) task force created with the sole purpose of solving cases of missing and murdered people along the Highway.

American serial killer *Roger Reece Kibbe* kills 17-year-old runaway and prostitute *Darcie Frackenpohl* in September of 1987. Most of Kibbe's bodies were dumped on the side of the Interstate 5 (I-5), one of the longest road systems in the United States.

Police discovered abandoned cars on the highway that belonged to some of the victims. At the time is was suspected that Kibbe patrolled the area searching out females with broken down cars. He became known as the I-5 Killer. The highways opened up *killing channels* for serial killers to move back forth between states.

Construction on the United State's highway systems began in 1956. In an act of congress known as the *Federal Aid Highway Act of 1956*. As of 2016, over 25% of all miles used by vehicles, use the interstates. Construction carried on through the 1950s, 1960s, 1970s and beyond.

They allowed potential serial killers to widen their geographical catchment area. They didn't have to stay in their home towns or States anymore and could just as easily drive to the next State over. Or even across the entire country if they wished.

Although hitchhiking was banned in almost all of the United States, many people were still using it as a form of travel. The more people that thumbed for rides on the country's interstates, the more potential victims there were for drifter killers.

The Bible Belt Strangler, also known as 'The Redhead Murders', were a series of unidentified murders linked to an unidentified serial killer. From 1978 to 1992. Their bodies were discovered along major highways across the States and they were thought to be hitchhikers or prostitutes. There is believed to be a total of six to 11 victims that have been attributed to one serial killer.

In most countries, the construction of these types of roads was one of the reasons why serial killing increased through the 1970s and reached a peak in the 1980s. Life was also made extremely difficult for law enforcement because of various State boundaries that existed.

It also meant that a serial killer's potential victim might not be recognised as such due to the then disconnected reporting between authorities. The highways provided an opportunity where there wasn't one before.

(II) The BTK Killer

(Previously available in 1978: Year of the Serial Killer.)

Born on March 9th, 1945, Denis Radar grew up in a normal household and went on to a happy marriage with children and a dream job at a security company. But Radar had been dreaming and having thoughts about restraining women so he could abuse and torture them. He killed from 1974 to 1991, and had killed at least ten people in that period.

His knowledge provided from the security job at ADT made it easier for him to cut the phone lines of his victim's homes. Around the time of the last murder in 1991, technology was on the rise. Computers were becoming more popular and more was known about technology,.

Denis Radar was one of the rare serial killers who it seemed wanted to become famous and it was Radar himself who created his own serial killing moniker. He would write letters to police and goad them constantly. He referred to himself as *The BTK Killer.* BTK standing for; 'Bind. Torture. Kill'.

On January 15th, 1974, Radar murdered four members of the *Otero* family in Wichita, Kansas. The parents and two children were murdered, the girl was 11-years-old and the boy was nine-years-old. Their bodies were discovered by the family's eldest child, *Charlie Otero*, as he returned home from school. It wasn't until Radar's arrest in 2005 when he would confess to the murders.

He claims that in October 1974, he wrote a letter that he stashed inside a book in the *Wichita Public Library*. It detailed the killing of the family. It was to be the start of his demand for media attention.

The following is a copy of a letter sent to a television station in 1978, it is displayed here as written with no editing. As such, the grammatical and spelling errors remain and are the style of Denis Radar.

"How many do I have to Kill before I get a name in the paper or some national attention. Do the cop think that all those deaths are not related? Golly -gee, yes the M.O. is different in each, but look a pattern is developing. The victims are tie up-most have been women-phone cut-bring some bondage mater sadist tendencies-no struggle, outside the death spot-no wintness except the Vain's Kids. They were very lucky; a phone call save them. I was go-ng to tape the boys and put plastics bag over there head like I did Joseph, and Shirley. And then hang the girl.

"God-oh God what a beautiful sexual relief that would been. Josephine, when I hung her really turn me on; her pleading for mercy then the rope took whole, she helpless; staring at me with wide terror fill eyes the rope getting tighter-tighter. You don't understand these things because your not underthe influence of factor x). The same thing that made Son of Sam, Jack the Ripper, Havery Glatman, Boston Strangler, Dr. H.H. Holmes Panty Hose Strangler OF Florida, Hillside Strangler, Ted of the West Coast and many more infamous character kill. Which seem s senseless, but we can't help it.

"There is no help, no cure, except death or being caught and put away. It a terrible nightmarebut, you see I don't lose any sleep over it. After a thing like Fox I ccome home and go about life like anyone else. And I will be like that until the urge hit me again. It not continuous and I don;t have *a lot of time. It take time to set a kill, one mistake and it all over. Since I about blew it on the phone-handwriting is out-letter guide is to long and typewriter can be traced too,.My short poem of death and maybe a drawing;later on real picture and maybe a tape of the sound will come your way. How will you know me. Before a murder or murders you will receive a copy of the initials B.T.K. , you keep that copy the original will show up some day on guess who?*

"May you not be the unluck one! P.S. How about some name for me, its time: 7 down and many more to go. I like the following How about you?

"THE B.T.K. STRANGLER', WICHITA STRANGLER', 'POETIC STRANGLER', 'THE BOND AGE STRANGLER' OR PSYCHO' THE WICHITA HANGMAN THE WICHITA EXECUTIONER, 'THE GAROTE PHATHOM', 'THE ASPHIXIATER'. B.T.K"

Radar was the perfect family man between murders, alluded to in a book written by his daughter, *Kerri Rawson*. She says that he was perceived as a pillar in the community and a family man who had a positive outlook on life with his wife and children.

We already know with *Ted Bundy* that some serial killers are capable of great love for women they hold in high esteem and yet capable of such violence towards those they don't.

Internally, Radar was holding off the desire to kille for months and sometimes years at a time. He would engage in autoerotic fantasies until the desire to kill became too strong.

The statement in the letter above proves that above all else, Radar was a narcissist and showed how much he craved attention. It is then assumed that he was fully aware of people's fascination with serial killers and the macabre, due in some part to the media putting serial killers in the limelight.

Radar confirmed later he knew the public would want to know more about him and they would want to know how he did it and what his motivations were. He was deliberately appealing to society's macabre appetite for murder.

In another letter to authorities he claimed he couldn't stop killing and society should be thankful to him for holding back the monster. In doing so, he suggested he should be thanked for holding back. He fantasised more and more about killing and held off by using the trophies of his victims in a sexual manner and masturbating.

He claimed to be seeking victims all the way through the late 1970s to the 1980s. His crimes became sexual in nature. In the killing of the Otero family, he used many methods. He strangled the father by putting a cord around his neck then he put a bag over nine-year-old Joseph Otero's head. He stranged the mother but she 'came back to life' and so he strangled her harder than before.

He killed the daughter, 11-year-old Josephine Otero last. He dragged her into the basement and tied a noose around her neck. Then he hung her and he watched her die in front of him all the while saying that she would be joining her family in heaven. Then he ripped off some of her clothing and masturbated over the girl's legs. He took many trophies from the scene.

The last murder was in January of 1991 when he murdered 62-year-old Dolores Davis. He claimed that as he had aged – he was 45-years-old when he killed Dolores – he had become weaker and as such needed weaker victims in order to kill.

He stalked Dolores before realising that she lived alone and seemed like a perfect victim. He was on a boy scout trip at the time and had left the campsite to kill her. He went to his parent's house and got changed into his '*killing clothes*' then drove to a church parking lot. He then walked to her house and broke in by smashing the window on the back door.

She came down and saw Radar waiting for her. He claimed Dolores said she was waiting for someone to arrive at her house shortly but it didn't stop him. He killed her and then used her own car to drive to a lake where he dumped her body. He then cleaned down the car, left it back at her house, returned home to get changed and went back to the boy scout camp as if nothing had happened.

In a twist of fate, it was Radar's obsession with himself and his desired celebrity status that caught him.

In one of his final letters to police, he asked if a floppy disk could be traced if he put confessions and writings onto one and sent it to them. The police answered in a newspaper ad in the *Wichita Eagle* stating that it would be safe and couldn't be traced. In 2005, he sent it in, along with an item of a victim's jewellery and a letter.

Police found some metadata in a deleted *Microsoft Word* document that included reference to a 'Dennis' and 'Christ Lutheran Church'. An internet search linked them as Radar was on the church council and along with other evidence compiled he was subsequently arrested. He finally got his wish as the Wichita Police announced that the BTK Killer had been caught.

He is currently serving ten consecutive life sentences at *El Dorado Correctional Facility* in Kansas.

(III) The Red Ripper

(Previously available in 1978: Year of the Serial Killer.)

Andrei Chikatilo, AKA: The Red Ripper was one of the most revered killers to have ever tarnished the Russian motherland. Almost all of his victims suffered sexual assault and mutilation resulting in the murders of 52 children and women. He did however confess to 56 murders.

He would share a bed with his mother, in fear of the war. But because of his constant bed-wetting, she would berate and beat him for it. He saw the direct results of Nazi occupation and was recorded as saying that he literally saw bodies being blown up into the air to fall down in a crumpled bloody mess to the dangerous streets below.

He did say that the sight of this both scared him and excited him. From this obvious and saturated exposure to things that no human should have seen, he started to develop images of torture in his head. His brother also befell a horrific fate.

"They caught my brother, who was only ten, they ate him, and sold some of his flesh for food."

Andrei Chikatilo, speaking of a group of Ukrainian men.

His first sexual experience was when he was 17-years-old, with a ten-year-old friend of his sister's. It was the first time he was able to ejaculate, he said he was able to do it with images of torture in his mind. He was normally shy around girls but had wrestled his sister's friend to the ground and forced himself upon her.

Because he couldn't physically rape her, he violently sexually assaulted her instead, a pre-cursor of things to come. After a series of embarrassments when girls his age started to question his impotence, he tried to hang himself in his mother's home but his mother and some neighbours helped to lift the noose off. With the feeling of nothing left in his life and the embarrassment of his failures, he moved away to a small town near *Rostov-on-don*.

Chikatilo went directly into the army but it didn't last long. When he returned home he tried many times to find a girlfriend But he was still unable to perform sexually and rumours started spreading again about his sexual inadequacies. He felt humiliated and dreamed about torturing the girls who were cruel to him.

He then went on to become a school teacher and did finally get married in a somewhat arranged marriage by his sister. Yet, it was not too long before his wife criticised everything he did, including his actions in the bedroom. He felt at that time that his life was a disaster and thus his torture fantasies increased.

His wife and mother criticised him constantly and he even tried to have children with his wife. It is said that he could only attempt conception by ejaculating onto his hands and then pushing it inside his wife.

When his mother died in 1973, he began abusing some of the girls in his school. It started with gentle touching and stroking but then his lust got the better of him and he began to grope and forcefully touch the girls. He said this made him feel powerful and he enjoyed the feeling it gave him.

Most of the time, the school covered it up with denial and lies instead of prosecution. Some would say that with hindsight, this allowed a pervert to become a killer.

It was December 22nd, 1978 and the killing of Yelena Zakotnova that would become the catalyst of further killings. Chikatilo later confirmed that he was only able to achieve orgasm through the stabbing of children and women and that the urge to relive the experience of Zakotnova was too overwhelming.

He claimed he didn't have to go looking for victims, he didn't have to seek them out. They were always right there and they were usually willing to follow him anywhere. It was however, another three years before he killed his second victim, 17-year-old *Larisa Tkachenko* who he lured to a forest to drink vodka.

Her body was found with mud in her mouth and she had been beaten and strangled to death. The body had been mutilated with a stick and Andrei's own teeth. He had also completely bitten off one of her nipples.

13-year-old *Lyubov Biryuk* was his third victim when he dragged her into the bushes from a secluded path. Her body was found with 22 knife wounds to the head, neck and pelvic region.

From then on, Chikatilo no longer attempted to resist the dark urges that were coming to him more often than he could control. He was free of any control and even the fear of being caught was lost on him. He had become a killer and nothing was going to stop him living out his fantasies.

He established a pattern, a plan of luring and killing children and young women in secluded areas. Most of the victims were runaways, prostitutes and homeless girls. They were easy to manipulate and gullible enough to do anything for a good drink.

For the next five victims and those that followed, each had evidence of mutilation to the eye sockets caused by a knife. In some cases, their eyes had been entirely gorged out and either allegedly eaten or disposed of somewhere else.

In 1982, he carried out a particularly horrific murder. Ten-year-old *Olga Stalmachenok* was lured to a cornfield on the outskirts of her town before she was brutally murdered. Her body was found a few days later. She had been stabbed 50 times in the head and body, her chest had been ripped open and he had cut out her lower bowel and uterus.

After having already brutally killed 15 children and young women, Chikatilo was arrested on suspicion of some of the murders, at least the ones that could be linked with the eye gorging signature. He had been spotted luring young girls away from bus stops and had a knife and rope in his bag when first arrested.

In 1984, Chikatilo was only one of 25,000 suspects, and details of the specifics of the crimes were sent to every police station in Russia. But the crimes were difficult to stomach, later victims appeared beheaded and so badly mutilated that one was even thought to have been caught in a harvesting machine.

The prime suspect became *Yuri Kalenik*, a 19-year-old who had lived in a home for mentally disabled children. He would return to the home to play games with the younger boys. The head nurse found him and another boy playing on the trolleys and accosted them. She then asked if they knew anything about the murders and the other boy said that *Yuri* was the killer.

Amazingly because of this soft accusation, the authorities believed they had broken the case and found the real killer. For the first few days after his arrest, he was beaten violently by investigators looking for a confession. Knowing that the only way to stop the beatings was to confess, Yuri gave a false confession.

Detective *Viktor Burakov* took over the investigation and changed direction with the case. Yuri's confession would one day be used as a basis for psychological false confession cases.

Yuri even managed to lead them to where the bodies were found, he did this by trying to understand what the police wanted of him. He even followed their direction when at one of the crime scenes. Burakov started to disbelieve Yuri's account but he was to remain in custody until it could be fully disproven.

Because Chikatilo had a strain of two blood types, he would constantly be discounted from the crimes. Many more brutal murders would take place. Before the Autumn of 1984, the investigation had attributed 24 victims to the unnamed murderer.

Semen found at each of the bodies matched up to blood type AB, yet every suspect who had that blood type was either found having an alibi or the incorrect personality match. The investigation was going out of control, the police and detectives knew nothing more than when they first started.

Chikatilo was then killing one victim every two weeks and the investigation could not work out how he was choosing his victims and why the evidence didn't seem to match up. The main issue was in the blood type against the original suspects list. It was the removal of that complete list that was causing the investigation to hit a dead end at every turn.

In August 1985 another body appeared near a small airport outside Moscow. Her body had been mutilated and exposed. Investigator Burakov went to Moscow to examine the victim and was in no doubt that it was the same killer.

Moscow detectives linked the killing of three young boys where one had been raped and one had been decapitated. At the same time, Burakov was called back to *Shakhty* where an 18-year-old girl was found dead with leaves stuffed into her mouth.

If any of this sounds slightly familiar, then you might have seen the film, *Child 44*, with *Gary Oldman* and *Tom Hardy*. The film is very loosely based on the Chikatilo murders.

On the girl's body they found the same blood type AB, red and blue thread under her fingernails and a single strand of grey hair. This was the most physical evidence found so far. Then the investigation brought in serial killer specialist, Chief Investigator *Issa Kostoyev*. Issa believed they had already come across the killer during their investigation but did not know it at the time. It was a low-blow to Burakov's investigation.

Issa began profiling the killer and used American profiling books that detailed cases of dismemberment and disfiguring of a killer's victims.

"Some killers were driven merely by arrogance and the idea that their victims were objects that belonged to them to do with as they pleased."

Serial killer specialist, Chief Investigator *Issa Kostoyev*

At this point in time, Issa discovered that Burakov's investigation had resulted in five false confessions, including that of Yuri Kalenik, who was still remanded in custody. Issa was furious and ordered all the information on all crime scenes to be compiled into one report and sent to everyone within the flawed investigation.

Then, having finally got hold of all the crime scene reports and known data, a *Dr. Bukhanovsky* spent months compiling a 65-page report on the suspect. He labelled the suspect; *Killer X*. He referred to Killer X as a necro-sadist, this would be someone who needed to watch people die in order to achieve sexual gratification.

He believed the multiple stabbing was a way to enter the victims sexually where the killer could not physically do so. The deepest cuts were representative of the height of his sexual pleasure. He even went as far as stating that Killer X mutilated or removed the eyes because he believed in the superstition that his image would be left on them.

Suddenly the investigation was picking up pace, with the report, the profiling and the evidence, they looked close to catching their killer. Then, just as suddenly as moral picked up again, the murders stopped and the investigation dried up. It would remain static for another *six* years.

Chikatilo had became wary and followed the investigation down to the most intimate detail. He held onto his urges somewhat and tried to change his methods of murder. He moved his killings away from Rostov-on-don to the Ukraine and further afield Ural towns in Russia, many of them were not ever linked to him at the time until after his confession.

It was six years later, in 1990, after the discovery of even more bodies linked to the same killer, a massive police operation got under way and a saturation of nearby bus stops, train stations and public gardens was evident by the amount of police acting as a deterrent. It was the biggest police investigation in Russia's history at the time. It seemed as though everyone had been involved at some point along the way.

On November 6th, 1990, Chikatilo killed his last victim, ending a serial killer's reign that began in 1978.

He was arrested coming out of a cafe after being watched actively seeking out young females to talk to and attempt to lure. They arrested Chikatilo and placed him in a cell with a gifted informant but he was not willing to admit or say anything against himself.

The next day, Kostoyev chose to handle the interrogation himself. It was a meeting of a serial killer and detective that some would fill their books with, such was the information that eventually came out of it. Chikatilo confessed to being a sexual deviant but for days never actually confessed to having anything to do with the murders.

A medical examination showed that Andrei Chikatilo's blood type was A which was different to the blood type found in his other bodily fluids. Chikatilo's semen had a very weak type B antibody making him a very rare case. But it would not have been enough to stand up in court should the entire investigation fall on his rare blood type.

They needed a real confession and it would be down to Dr. Bukhanovsky to finally get the confession from him. Dr. Bukhanovsky agreed to question him but only out of a professional interest and not from a legal standpoint.

Chikatilo would later say that he gave up everything to Dr. Bukhanovsky because he seemed to be the only person who ever really understood him. Finally, he broke down and admitted that he had done everything and more.

It was immediately apparent that the initial number of 36 victims was going to be a long way off the final number. Chikatilo remembered the details of each of his murders and would go through them in turn, one by one. He would never stick to a pattern, sometimes he would learn someone's walking routes, yet other times would be opportunistic killings. He would squat beside the bodies and cut them so as not to get blood on his clothes.

Chikatilo would sometimes place his semen inside a uterus that he had just removed. Then as he walked along a path, he would chew on it. He never admitted to ingesting the remains but no missing body parts were ever found.

"The cries, the blood and the agony gave me relaxation and a certain pleasure."

Andrei Chikatilo, in his confession.

He claimed the reason for mutilating or cutting out his victim's eyes was because he had initially believed an old urban legend that the image of a murderer is left imprinted on the eyes of the victim. It confirmed the same fact that had been written in Dr. Bukhanovsky's report.

He had enjoyed playing with the blood of his victims and confessed to tearing at the victim's genitalia, nipples, tongues and lips with his teeth. He chewed upon the uterus of his female victims and the testicles of his few male victims. But he still maintained that he never ate them, he simply chewed and discarded.

He was found guilty of 52 murders and sentenced to death for each and every one.

In 1992, another Russian serial killer, *Alexander Pichushkin,* came to the fore. Upon his arrest in 2006, he talks about Andrei Chikatilo in his own confessions. He claimed that he wanted to kill *more* than Chikatilo and some say he might have succeeded.

For it is a dark part of human nature that when one serial killer is captured, there will always be another in the shadows, awaiting his or her time in the spotlight.

(IV) The Golden State Killer

(Previously available in 1978: Year of the Serial Killer.)

Not since *Ted Bundy* has the case of a serial killer been so widely spoken about in media and especially in online forums. His capture brings to end one of the largest serial killing mysteries of the Twentieth Century.

At the time of editing this book, Joseph James DeAngelo has had DNA evidence linking him to 13 murders. As the trial is in the early stages, we would expect the confirmed death toll to rise.

We can talk about it now because police have confirmed that the DNA is a 100% match for DeAngelo and his victims. That he is refusing to talk about it is becoming irrelevant as his innocence has already been stripped away from him.

It is a complicated case with so many threads of crime coming to a head. *The Golden State Killer* was a serial killer, rapist and burglar who killed at least 13 people, committed more than 50 rapes, and over 100 burglaries in California from 1974 to 1986.

Each of his known three crime sprees afforded him a new moniker in the media. This was before it became evident that the three moniker's were one and the same person. So along with the Golden State Killer, which is what the press are currently running with, he was also the *East*

Area Rapist (EAR) and the *Original Night Stalker* (ONS).

It has also been suggested that there are links to him being the *Diamond Knot Killer, The Cordova Cat, The Rippon Court Shooter,* and *The Visalia Ransacker.*

On February 2nd, 1978, DeAngelo shot dead *Brian Maggiore* and *Katie Maggiore.* DNA has been matched against the two victims and the killer is confirmed to be DeAngelo. It is claimed by one witness that he had already killed 14 people before 1974 and it is an assumption that he killed again in 1978, probably more than once.

It's important to note that DeAngelo's DNA is a 100% match for him being the East Area Rapist, The Original Night Stalker, and the Golden State Killer.

He was identified through a DNA match with his fourth cousin on an open data personal genomics website. Subsequently, the investigators built a family tree and zoned in on DeAngelo based on living locations, age at the time of the crimes, and serial killer profiling techniques. They secretly gained access to his DNA from a throw-away item as they were watching him and it came back to be a 100% match.

DeAngelo's father served in World War Two but not much is known about him beyond that. After his parents divorce, his mother quickly remarried and they moved to California from New York. His childhood and developing years were formed by his father returning from war, divorce and displacement of his home life.

In 1964, he joined the U.S Navy and was subsequently deployed to Vietnam. We've already spoken in this book about the toxic legacy of World War Two and the damaging effect of Vietnam on serving soldiers but divorce also plays a major factor.

In most of the rape cases, the crimes took place too long ago and cannot be tried in a court of law due to the statute of limitations. However, in their place, he is being charged with kidnapping.

In June, 1972, he garnered a Bachelors Degree in Criminal Justice at the *California State University* and subsequently joined the *Exeter Police Department* in 1973. He was promoted to sergeant and it is suggested that he was using the department as a stepping stone to becoming an FBI Agent.

Whilst working on the force, he was already operating as the *Visalia Ransacker*. If witness statements are to be believed he had already killed many people by that point in time.

He then moved from the Exeter Department to the *Auburn Police Department* in 1976. June 1976, is the first confirmed attack of the East Area Rapist. In 1978, under the same moniker, he moved onto murder. The last known attack of his East Area Rapist name was on July 5th, 1979, in Danville, California.

He was then fired from the Auburn Police Department for shoplifting in a *Pay & Save* store. If we base the assumption that DeAngelo had joined the police in order to use it as a stepping stone to the FBI, then his dismissal from the Auburn PD would have put to bed any chance he ever had to work with the FBI.

October 1st 1979, is the date of the first attack attributed to the Original Night Stalker (ONS). The more famously known Night Stalker was *Richard Ramirez* who killed 14 people from 1984 to 1985.

On December 30th 1979, *Dr. Robert Offerman* and *Alexandria Manning* are killed in their home near Goleta, 100 miles northwest of Los Angeles.

Just three months later another double murder takes place in Ventura. *Lyman* and *Charlene Smith* are bound and bludgeoned to death with a fireplace log. Charlene had been sexually assaulted and tied with a curtain cord. Their 12-year-old son found their bodies three days later. DNA collected from this scene was used to identify DeAngelo almost 40 years later.

On August 21st, 1980, *Keith* and *Patti Harrington* of Laguna Niguel, California, were bludgeoned to death. Some sources bizarrely put this five years earlier but it was in fact 1980. Keith's father discovered their beaten bodies when he arrived for dinner on the Thursday night. There were more murders in the same area and it wasn't until September of 1981 that the killings stopped, for a while.

In September of that year, DeAngelo's first child was born in Sacramento. As we've discussed with *Ted Bundy*, some serial killers hold their own family in higher esteem than others. This might seem like a given notion but some serial killers are able to lift up their wives and children as being important to them, they respect and revere their own families. At the same they focus any hatred they might have garnered towards them on other females or children.

It's important because after DeAngelo's first child, there is an assumed five year gap where no crimes were committed. It wasn't until the May 4th 1986, murder of *Janelle Cruz* in Irvine, that the investigation would start linking DeAngelo to the new spate of murders and rapes.

His second child is born in 1986 and the third in 1989. Beyond that, there are no crimes committed and some put this down to the fact he now had children of his own and was intent on raising his family.

He was arrested in July 2012 for driving under the influence. Little did the officers know they had one of the most notorious killers and rapists in their custody. It wasn't until March 2018 when he became a suspect due to a DNA match to his fourth cousin on a DNA database and then arrested in April 2018.

Which raises the important notion of *genetic informants*.

You didn't really think those ancestry DNA sites were just to find out more about your own family, did you? Mostly they are, of course, but they are being used to a massive extent in the investigation of cold cases and new cases.

You could unwittingly be a genetic informant and not ever know it. The rise of the genetic informant is something for debate in further discussions.

Police are currently investigating further crimes beyond 1986 to find a link between them and DeAngelo. As of 2019 they have not confirmed anything conclusive. DeAngelo still hasn't admitted anything to the investigation, even though the DNA evidence is conclusive.

There is a theory that he was also the *Zodiac Killer* but there has been no evidence pointing towards it at the present time, even though some of his killings were similar in style.

Joseph James DeAngelo is initially being charged with the murders of 13 people but is accused of many more. He is also accused of over 50 rapes, kidnappings and burglaries across six counties in California. The death penalty is being sought in what could be a very lengthy trial.

All facts formulated as of July 2019.

(V) Bibliography

Citations, data, and suggested reading.

A. Nortje, C. G. Tredoux, K. Kempen and A. Vredeveldt. (2013) "Applying Laboratory Techniques to a Real-Life Case: What Insight can we Provide about the Station Strangler Case?" American Psychology-Law Society.

Disaster Center Crime Data. (Retrieved 2019) http://www.disastercenter.com/crime. DCC.

Aamodt, M. G. (2016). Serial killer statistics. Retrieved June 2019 from http://maamodt.asp.radford.edu Radford University.

Aamodt, M. G., & Moyse, C. (2003) Researching the multiple murderer: A comprehensive bibliography of books on specific serial, mass, and spree killers. *Journal of Police and Criminal Psychology,* 18(1).

Bartels, K. (1998). Serial Killers: Sublimity to Be Continued. Aesthetics and Criminal History. Amerikastudien / American Studies, 43(3), 497-516.

Branson, Allan. (2013). African American Serial Killers: Over-Represented Yet Under-acknowledged. The Howard Journal of Criminal Justice. 52.

Brunt, Martin. Sky News. (2008) "Ex-Detective Held Over Axe Murder"..

https://news.sky.com/skynews/Home/Sky-News-Archive/Article/20080641313539 Sky.com News Archive.

CBS Sacramento. (2016). "California Inmate On Death Row Since 1988 Dies In The Hospital" https://sacramento.cbslocal.com/2016/12/14/california-inmate-on-death-row-since-1988-dies-in-the-hospital/. CBS.

Chen, Edwin. Los Angeles Times. (April 27th 1989). "Man Convicted of 4 Murders; 2 Linked to Southside Slayer Case." https://www.latimes.com/archives/la-xpm-1989-04-27-me-1912-story.html. Latimes.com

Cohen, M. (1997). Inside the Murderer. Studies in Popular Culture, 19(3), 49-63.

Conrath, R. (1994). The Guys Who Shoot to Thrill: Serial Killers and the American Popular Unconscious. Revue Française D'études Américaines, (60), 143-152.

Dahl, G., & DellaVigna, S. (2009). Does Movie Violence Increase Violent Crime? The Quarterly Journal of Economics, 124(2), 677-734.

Disaster Center Crime Data. (Retrieved 2019) http://www.disastercenter.com/crime. DCC.

Dodd, Vikram. Guardian, The. (2014). Cherry Groce inquest: officer takes full blame for shot that led to Brixton riots https://www.theguardian.com/uk-news/2014/jul/01/cherry-groce-inquest-officer-takes-blame-shooting-brixton-riots Guardian.com.

Dresser, R. (2011). At law: Families and Forensic DNA Profiles. The Hastings Center Report, 41(3), 11-12.

E. G. L. (1919). The Statute of Limitations and the Conflict of Laws. The

Yale Law Journal, 28(5), 492-498.

Federal Bureau of Investigation. (2008). Serial Murder: Multi-disciplinary Perspectives for Investigators. Washington, DC. U.S. Department of Justice.

Federal Bureau of Investigation. (2009). Highway serial killing database release. https://archives.fbi.gov/archives/news/stories/2009/april/highwayseri al_040609. U.S Department of Justice.

Fox, J., & Levin, J. (1998). Multiple Homicide: Patterns of Serial and Mass Murder. Crime and Justice, 23, 407-455.

Foy, D. (1987). Disasters at Sea and their Prevention. RSA Journal, 136(5377), 13-24.

Friedrichsen, Gisela. (1995) Criminal Justice. https://www.spiegel.de/spiegel/print/d-9247676.html Der Spiegel 52/1995.

Ganesan, N., & Kim, S. (Eds.). (2013). State Violence in East Asia. University Press of Kentucky.

Godwin, M., (2008) (2nd Edition). Hunting Serial Predators. Jones & Bartlett Publishers, MA.

Gorman, Anna. (2004). "Ten Murder Charges Filed." Retrieved 2019. Los Angeles Times.

Guardian, The. (2012). Terry Waite returns to Lebanon 25 years after kidnapping https://www.theguardian.com/world/2012/dec/09/terry-waite-returns-lebanon-kidnapping?CMP=share_btn_tw. Theguardian.com

Hans Gross, (1907, retrieved 2019) Criminal Investigation: A Practical Handbook for Magistrates, Police Officers and Lawyers.

Havill, Adrian. (2001). Born Evil: A True Story of Cannibalism and Serial Murder. New York, N.Y.: St. Martin's Press. Retrieved 2019.

Jarvis, C., (March 20th, 1997). "Academic sleuth made startling predictions". News & Observer, Raleigh, NC.

Kandel, Jason, (2011). "Police tie Grim Sleeper suspect to six more killings." https://www.reuters.com/article/us-crime-grimsleeper/police-tie-grim-sleeper-suspect-to-six-more-killings-idUSTRE7A20L120111103. Reuters.

Keenan, Thomas, 'Getting the Dead to Tell Me what Happened: Justice, Prosopopoeia, and Forensic Afterlives', in Forensic Architecture, ed., Forensic, 35-55.

LAPD Online. (Retrieved July 2019) Photos of Grim Sleeper Victims. http://www.lapdonline.org/grimsleeper. Lapdonline.com

Leskanic, T., (2004) "Inmate indicted in 1995 killing." Retrieved 2019. Fayetteville Observer.

Lodinews. (2016) "Convicted killer Loren Herzog commits suicide." Lodinews.com. http://www.lodinews.com/news/article_64587e42-4122-11e1-b68e-001871e3ce6c.html

Meija, Brittny. Los Angeles Times. (Nov 9th 2015). Grim Sleeper: Defense backtracks on expert witness https://www.latimes.com/local/lanow/la-me-ln-grim-sleeper-defense-backtracks-expert-witness-20151109-story.htm.l Retrieved 2019. latimes.com

Miller, G. (2010). Familial DNA Testing Scores A Win in Serial Killer Case. Science, 329(5989), new series, 262-262.

Montgomery, Ben. Zayas, Alexandra. (July 8th 2007). "Valley murder victims." Concord Monitor. Archived from the original in 2015. Concordmonitor.com.

Nelson, Harold E. (1987). NIST Interagency/Internal Report (NISTIR) – 87-3560. May 29th.

NSQCCA 327. (1999), Regina v Rose [1999]. New South Wales Criminal Court of Appeal. No. 60520 of 1998

Oakley, Ben. Luisa, Marina. (2019) Mentacracy: Living under the Rule of Mental Illness. United Kingdom. Twelvetrees Publishing

Pelisek, Christine (2007). "Death Penalty for Chester Turner". LA Weekly. Village Voice Media. Rtvd 2019. http://www.laweekly.com/2007-05-17/news/death-penalty-for-chester-turner/

Ram, N. (2011). Fortuity and Forensic Familial Identification. Stanford Law Review, 63(4), 751-812.

Robinson, Kathleen. (2012). "Puerto Rico fire is the second-deadliest hotel fire in U.S. history." NFPA Journal, November/December 2012.

Schildcrout, J. (2014). Murder Most Queer: The Homicidal Homosexual in the American Theater. Ann Arbor: University of Michigan Press.

Seltzer, M. (1995). Serial Killers (II): The Pathological Public Sphere. Critical Inquiry, 22(1), 122-149.

Smith, C., Lobban, G., O'Loughlin, M. (Eds.) (2013). Psychodynamic Psychotherapy in South Africa: Contexts, theories and applications. Johannesburg: Wits University Press.

Susan L. Murray PhD, PE, Matthew S. Thimgan PhD, (2016). "Human Fatigue Risk Management."

Times, Los Angeles, (Retrieved 2019). "Guilty verdicts in Grim Sleeper serial killer case." https://www.latimes.com/local/lanow/la-me-ln-grim-sleeper-death-verdict-20160606-snap-story.html. latimes.com.

Trevor A. Kletz DSc, FEng, FIChemE, FRSC, (1990). Critical Aspects of Safety and Loss Prevention.

Walker, J., (1997). The Traumatic Paradox: Documentary Films, Historical Fictions, and Cataclysmic Past Events. Signs, 22(4), 803-825.

www.benoakley.co.uk

'Thank you for reading and coming along for the ride! I hope you had as much fun as I did. If you have time to spare then a short review would be hugely appreciated.'

Visit Ben Oakley to discover new stories, find out more about the author and make contact. Make sure to follow Ben Oakley on the book site of your choice.